How to Use the Internet to Get Your Next Job

By Janet Nagle

With Foreword by Donna Fitzgerald, Owner and CEO of Contemporaries, Inc., Staffing Agency

With Preface by Nathan W. Egan, Founder and Managing Partner of Freesource, LLC

HOW TO USE THE INTERNET TO GET YOUR NEXT JOB

Library of Congress Cataloging-in-Publication Data

Nagle, Janet, 1959-
  How to use the Internet to get your next job / Janet Nagle.
      p. cm.
  Includes bibliographical references and index.
  ISBN-13: 978-1-60138-239-9 (alk. paper)
  ISBN-10: 1-60138-239-1 (alk. paper)
  1. Job hunting--Computer network resources. 2. Résumés (Employment)--Computer network resources. 3. Internet. I. Title.
  HF5382.7.N34 2010
  650.140285'4678--dc22

                                        2009051258

Printed in the United States

PROJECT MANAGER: Nicole Orr • norr@atlantic-pub.com
PEER REVIEWER: Marilee Griffin • mgriffin@atlantic-pub.com
INTERIOR DESIGN: Samantha Martin • smartin@atlantic-pub.com
ASSISTANT EDITOR: • Angela Pham • apham@atlantic-pub.com

We recently lost our beloved pet "Bear," who was not only our best and dearest friend but also the "Vice President of Sunshine" here at Atlantic Publishing. He did not receive a salary but worked tirelessly 24 hours a day to please his parents. Bear was a rescue dog that turned around and showered myself, my wife, Sherri, his grandparents Jean, Bob, and Nancy, and every person and animal he met (maybe not rabbits) with friendship and love. He made a lot of people smile every day.

We wanted you to know that a portion of the profits of this book will be donated to The Humane Society of the United States. *–Douglas & Sherri Brown*

The human-animal bond is as old as human history. We cherish our animal companions for their unconditional affection and acceptance. We feel a thrill when we glimpse wild creatures in their natural habitat or in our own backyard.

Unfortunately, the human-animal bond has at times been weakened. Humans have exploited some animal species to the point of extinction.

The Humane Society of the United States makes a difference in the lives of animals here at home and worldwide. The HSUS is dedicated to creating a world where our relationship with animals is guided by compassion. We seek a truly humane society in which animals are respected for their intrinsic value, and where the human-animal bond is strong.

Want to help animals? We have plenty of suggestions. Adopt a pet from a local shelter, join The Humane Society and be a part of our work to help companion animals and wildlife. You will be funding our educational, legislative, investigative and outreach projects in the U.S. and across the globe.

Or perhaps you'd like to make a memorial donation in honor of a pet, friend or relative? You can through our Kindred Spirits program. And if you'd like to contribute in a more structured way, our Planned Giving Office has suggestions about estate planning, annuities, and even gifts of stock that avoid capital gains taxes.

Maybe you have land that you would like to preserve as a lasting habitat for wildlife. Our Wildlife Land Trust can help you. Perhaps the land you want to share is a backyard— that's enough. Our Urban Wildlife Sanctuary Program will show you how to create a habitat for your wild neighbors.

So you see, it's easy to help animals. And The HSUS is here to help.

THE HUMANE SOCIETY OF THE UNITED STATES®

2100 L Street NW • Washington, DC 20037 • 202-452-1100
www.hsus.org

SPECIAL THANKS

Most successful projects do not happen overnight and are not complete without unique assistance and guidance from others. This book is no exception.

I'd like to thank my Dad, first and foremost, for teaching me to love books and to appreciate their tremendous value.

I would also like to thank both Amanda Miller and Nicole Orr at Atlantic Publishing; Amanda for allowing me to run with her great vision for the project, and Nicole for her assistance in making the book even better.

A very special thanks to Donna Fitzgerald, Contemporaries, Inc. owner, whose insight, knowledge, unending advice, and guidance helped move a good idea and dream into reality for the betterment of all job seekers.

I'd also like to thank Rory Bledsoe for her special assistance in the project. As a recent graduate of Rice University, Rory provided valuable insight into how to secure a position by utilizing the Internet. To my case study participants: A deep appreciation and thanks for sharing your thoughts, experiences, and inspiration in an effort to help others. To people like Emily Phillips of Met Life, thank you so much for following through. To Sara Harris: A special thanks for your support. To Mike Benavidez: Thanks for coming through in a clutch. To Lily: We will always love and remember you.

A special thanks to my daughter, Samantha, who had to endure, and finally, to my friends at the San Antonio Pug Rescue, Deb and Kathleen, a definite, "I owe you," for helping my little guys and me when it truly counted. The two of you do wonderful things for the lost little Pugs of Texas, and I hope you continue your great work for years to come.

TABLE OF CONTENTS

Chapter 4: Getting Organized
For Your Internet Job Search   87

Chapter 5: Using Internet Resources for Résumés, Cover Letters, and Other Items   111

Chapter 9: Reduce Cyber Crime by Preventing Strangers From Entering Your Virtual Life   215

Chapter 10: Getting Hired —
Moving Closer to Success   235

Chapter 11: Conclusion — What to do
After You Have Been Hired   251

Appendix A: Big-Name Sites, Search Engines, Niche Sites, and Job Boards   259

Appendix B: Federal and Other Government Job Sites   263

Appendix C: Résumé Help and Cover Letter Samples   267

FOREWORD

As someone who has worked in the staffing industry for over 20 years, I can say with confidence that I possess insider knowledge when it comes to hiring the right people, knowing what goes into making a quality match between a company and candidate, and knowing what people are doing to get a job. As a staffing expert in the Boston area and some one who has owned my own staffing firm for eleven years, I have seen it all — especially the mistakes people continually make when it comes to applying for jobs. Furthermore, I know first-hand what makes a job candidate stand out with a recruiter and what necessary actions they need to take in order to ensure they move on to the next level in the hiring process. Janet Nagle's book, *How to Use the Internet to Get Your Next Job*, will give job seekers the edge they need in this incredibly competitive market.

Eleven years ago, the staffing and employment industry was completely different, largely due to the lack of high-end technology. When I first started, we did not utilize the Internet at all. Our business was all done via the telephone, whether it was the client who called to place an order for a temporary employee, or a job candidate who called to let us know they were going to fax or snail mail his or her résumé after seeing a Contemporaries, Inc., advertisement. The fact that everything was done by phone and paper made the process much slower and largely limited our candidate pool.

In order to attract the most highly qualified candidates, we would publish advertisements in the Yellow Pages and local newspapers, and we would post listings to local colleges and universities. Due to the format of this process, we were not able to screen out candidates very easily. In some ways, this meant that a potential candidate had a better shot in terms of getting an interview; a single mistake on his or her résumé or cover letter would not filter them out of the process because we first had to speak them — it was still a personalized process.

Eleven years later, hiring methods and procedures have changed drastically — 98 percent of our candidates now come through the Internet. There is also an approximate ratio of 25:1 in terms of the number of résumés we receive daily for each job listing. The business is constantly evolving as a result of the new technology.

There are many ways a candidate can impress a potential employer, and just as many ways that they can decrease their chances of being considered. Candidates need to arm themselves with the knowledge presented in this book if they are going to find a job and get hired.

They also need to know their way around the Internet because it has become the main avenue in which job searches and connections between employers and candidates are made. This is why this book is so essential — it can help job seekers learn how to set themselves apart in this ultra competitive pool of candidates. You need a wealth of valuable resources at your disposal in order to know exactly what a hiring manager is looking for and how to make the connection to secure the position. *How to Use the*

Internet to Get Your Next Job is one of these resources that can make the difference between whether you are considered for a position, and whether the job goes to someone else with skills very similar to your own. I would highly recommend this book to anyone who is serious about finding his or her next job through the Internet.

Donna Fitzgerald,
Owner and CEO of Contemporaries, Inc., Staffing Agency

Boston, Massachusetts
55 Court Street Suite 330
Boston, MA 02108
Phone 617-723-9797
Fax 617-723-4140

PREFACE

I have helped thousands of people get jobs; it might be safe to say I have helped more than 25,000 people. And yet, I was never a recruiter. Never a hiring manager. Never even worked in human resources. Never was a career coach, nor was I a résumé writer.

So how did I do it? I did it over the Internet.

I sold a revolutionary software program to companies that forever changed the game of talent acquisition. Delivered in a SaaS format (Software as a Service), I was responsible for selling LinkedIn's upgraded Corporate Solutions recruiting product suite, now called "Talent Advantage." I was one of the first sales reps on the East Coast, and I sold it to some of the most significant employers in the world. In nine short months, we had grown to be recognized as the world's premier social media consulting firm, with clients like Forbes, Mandarin Oriental, and NYC & Company.

Over the last 2-3 years, Web services have completely redefined the landscape for recruiters and job seekers. In fact, it represents the biggest sea-change in technology that business, as a whole, will see in our lifetime.

What I am getting to here is this: The service-based Internet is the most important thing you can learn for managing your personal brand and landing your next big job.

Keeping that in mind, I'd like to tell you a true story about how the Internet is changing careers, connections, and lives. It's about me and my friend Mark Schaefer.

Back in 2008, I had an idea to start a company that assembled all of the free Internet technologies in a way that would help companies dramatically reduce costs and improve performance. It's called Freesource, and I immediately hit the road to start talking about it.

After a brilliant corporate career, Mark had also just started his own consulting company, Schaefer Marketing Solutions. He was looking to learn as much as he could about the emerging Internet trends, saw a notice of my seminar, and attended.

He liked what he heard and started following me on Twitter. Even through these little 140-character messages, I could tell Mark was an interesting guy. He skillfully nurtured his relationship with me, and with other potential business partners. On his LinkedIn profile, I was able to view his detailed background and accomplishments, and I realized there was a lot we could learn from each other. I also started reading his blog and could see we thought alike on many issues.

Remember, this all started with the Internet — not a résumé, and certainly not an ad in a newspaper.

The way Mark and I connected and grew together is how much of the business world works these days. If he had simply sent a résumé or made a cold call, we probably never would have grown into this dynamic partnership, but through the Internet, we were able to "pre-populate" our business relationship.

It goes to show that the professional image you have in the real world, the one you manage every day, does not just "show up" in the virtual world. In fact, the translation is terrible unless you work to make it happen. Is your online job search optimized? Are you doing everything you can to land your dream job?

Did you know that you can use Twitter to create a relationship with a company that you want to work for? Did you know there are niche-specific job search engines available to help you find job openings in your industry? Did you know you can self-assess your skills and strengths with online applications? Did you know that your LinkedIn profile can be a beacon for personal brand, attracting recruiters to you and interfacing with potential employers — even while you are asleep at night? Did you know the key to all of this is knowing how to differentiate yourself online?

Janet Nagle's *How to Use the Internet to Get Your Next Job* tells you how. The Internet has turned many business processes on its head, including talent acquisition. You've bought Nagle's book to learn how to find a job through the Internet. That's a powerful first step. Here's the next one: Don't just study this book and her Web-based strategies — immerse yourself in them.

Master personal branding and applying for jobs through the Internet and you will have recruiters calling *you*.

Cheers and best regards,

Nathan W. Egan
Founder + Managing Partner
Freesource, LLC

www.freesourceagency.com
http://twitter.com/nathanegan
http://linkedin.com/in/nathanegan

INTRODUCTION

Job Searching in a Virtual World

The sun is shining — there is not a cloud in the sky as you leap out of bed, full of hope and promise. Smiling confidently in the mirror, you just know today is going to be the day you find that dream job you have been longing for.

Dressed and ready to go, you skip breakfast. You will pick something up at Starbucks®, your makeshift office for this morning. You do your last check before you leave the house. Red marker? Yes. Pens? Yes. Folder full of résumés? Yes. Cell phone? Yes. Note pad? Yes. That is all you need. Well-armed, shoulders back, chin up high, you walk out of the house ready to conquer the world.

You tuck the local and national newspapers under your arm when they call your order for a large — Venti® — coffee. You are going to need all the caffeine you can consume today if you are going to land that job. You forgo your favorite overstuffed couch, sliding into one of the stiff-back chairs opposite a little table tucked in the corner instead. You cannot get too comfortable. You have big business to attend to; you are making a major move toward ensuring a prosperous future for yourself.

Your spirits are high as you barely scan the front page of the day's local newspaper. That is not where you are going to find your high-paying, tremendously rewarding new job that fits you like a woolen glove. You are on a mission with the classifieds to find your dream job. No sense wasting time on the "For Sale" items, pets, and lease properties. It is straight over to the "Help Wanted" section.

You are slightly disappointed with the skimpy size of the printed sheets. You did expect to pour over page after page. Well, no problem. It will make the hunt for a job even easier. All you have to do is find one or two interesting advertisements – which match your own high standards – and you are off and running.

With blue pen and red marker poised at the ready, you read on and take aim.

After eating your banana nut muffin and drinking a second — and then third — cup of coffee, you glance at your watch and are stunned to find that hours have gone by. Worse yet, you are no closer to landing that dream job than you were when you woke up this morning. "Have I really been here that long?" you ask yourself.

With a heavy sigh, you gather your coat and materials and head for the door. Your crumpled newspaper pages look as if they have just returned from the battlefield. Using a blue pen to circle job ad after job ad, one by one, they all fall victim to the dreaded red slasher. Some were nixed because you did not have the right skills, or the company was too far out of your comfort zone. Still, others met the same fate because there was not enough information about them, or the pay was too low, and so on and so on.

Your brilliantly crafted résumés seem like leftover candy on the day after Halloween: It feels like you bought the best goodies in the neighborhood, but you ended up spending the night without a single trick-or-treater knocking on your door.

Outside of the coffee and muffin, the time was basically a waste. You could have stayed for lunch, but you had already run out of job leads long before. As you head home, you shake your head, thinking, "There just has to be a better way to find a job."

Well, lucky for you, there is a much better way; it is called the Internet. It is fully loaded with job listings and postings that may rival your own imagination, when it comes to dream jobs. Whether it is a particular company, a government agency, or an occupation that you just know is right for you, the sky is the limit. In the time it took you to comb over the newspapers and decide there was nothing of value, you could have found the right job listing, applied for it, sent your résumé, and still had time to hit the gym, if you wanted. In fact, you could have already landed an interview and started prepping for it. Life and opportunities move very fast on the Internet.

Rather than depending on conventional methods, the Internet is a much swifter means for finding hundreds of great job leads. In addition, if you know how to navigate through the World Wide Web, you can apply for a position in a matter of minutes. The Internet is truly a marvel for job seekers, especially considering the fact that if you applied to a job posting through a newspaper, it would take days for your résumé and cover letter to reach a potential employer. Now, with a few select clicks on your computer, your résumé could be in the hands of your next potential boss before you can say "Non-fat, iced, vanilla latte."

For a job seeker, the Internet can be a ticket to anywhere in the world. You can literally apply for a position in almost any country without ever leaving your home. Through the Internet, employers will also get to know you without ever having set eyes on you. Because your first contact with a potential employer will be virtual, through the Internet, you will need to know the ins and outs, along with the highlights and pitfalls — so strap yourself in and get ready for the ride that will change your life forever.

CHAPTER 1

How the Internet Changed the Process

Internet Lingo

E-mail: A form of communication through the Internet where you can send a message to an individual or a group of individuals. The e-mail itself is usually word- or text-based, but you can also send pictures, graphics, and other items as well.

Online job listings (postings): Job advertisements that can be found on the Internet. The listings or postings usually provide information about a particular job and usually include a description of the job, as well as instructions on how and where to apply for the position.

Online job site: An Internet site where numerous jobs can be found and applied for. There are sites for specific types of jobs, or for specific types of employers, like **www.usajobs.gov**, which is the federal government's official site for job postings and employment information.

Search engine: An Internet entity that assists users by finding information posted in different locations on the World Wide Web. It allows users to access the information in a concise manner, without forcing the user to consult several different places or sites. As it pertains to a job search, a search engine is a site that collects job titles, job descriptions, job postings, and employer information.

Previously, you could pretty much tell the importance of a position by the size of the job advertisement, as well as where it was found. For example, an advertisement for a marketing professional listed in *The New York Times* or *The Wall Street Journal* was likely to pay more than a job being advertised in a free flier that you may have picked up at the local supermarket or from a corner vending machine.

Of course, you would have to read the newspapers or know where to find the free flier in order to find out about the position and apply for the job, and if you did not happen to buy the newspaper on the particular day or days the ad was run, then you were out of luck. Likewise, your luck was limited if you used a staffing agency, where you could only apply to the clients and positions the employment agency had available to them. Job seekers had to pound the pavement if they were going to find the most lucrative positions in their own communities — and if they were looking to move to another state, the options were even fewer. New technology has changed that.

The U.S. Census Bureau reports that 62 percent of households across the country access the Internet at home as of 2007, an increase of 18 percent from 1997. With more than half of the homes in the country using the Internet, the door is open for job seekers to apply for jobs within the comfort of their own homes. Where previously limited by location, a job seeker in California can now view, search, and apply for jobs in New York, Massachusetts, or even Europe — it is as simple as finding an online job posting and submitting a résumé the same day.

But traditional methods still apply, too. There are still ads to sift through, staffing agencies to reference, companies to visit, and chances to network. The difference, however, is that most of this is now done online. Job seekers can search for a particular company Web site or browse listings on a staffing agency's Web site. In addition, job seekers can also use online social networks to find job leads, or to make professional acquaintances online.

You need to be on a level playing field — there are millions of other candidates who are visiting the same sites, and viewing and applying for the same jobs as you. Otherwise, your competitor will get the job. But first, you should understand why the Internet offers endless job opportunities, and how it has changed the face of the game.

Finding a Job in Any Economy

Employers and job seekers are turning to the Internet, more than ever before, as a main resource for job searching and candidate hiring. When the economy is tough, a successful job search may mean the difference between finding a job quickly or spending months being unemployed. The Internet has proved itself a viable link among employers, jobs, and candidates, and the convenience the Internet presents means that it is here to stay as a valuable employment resource — for job seekers and employers alike.

An increase in unemployment

The unemployment rate for the United States was 10.2 percent in October 2009, according to the U.S. Department of Labor. In terms of people, the number translates into about 15.7 million without jobs. Of those individuals, hundreds, thousands, and even millions were conducting active job searches on a daily basis. These unemployment numbers, despite some fluctuation, steadily increased since January 2008, when the rate was 4.9 percent. In just a year, there was a considerable difference in the number of lost jobs and unemployed workers, according to the same government agency source. Numerous positions were lost as employers cut back, downsized, or went out of business. At times, thousands of positions were lost on a monthly basis. Although an employee who was not meeting job standards was always in danger of being let go, the same could now be said for the outstanding employee under the trend of downsizing and restructuring.

For a job seeker, the news does seem pretty grim. However, the situation can also provide more incentive to ensure that you, as the job seeker, are in the best possible position in terms of having high-quality tools.

The Internet can help job seekers locate new jobs, in addition to helping the same individuals uncover skills they may not be aware they even possess. Such newfound skills may be perfect for another occupation the job seeker has not already thought about. Being versatile and having an abundance of skills and marketable qualities can also be the type of advantage that moves a job candidate from being a possible contender to actually being hired.

The job hunt when the economy is good

You may see even more positions posted when the economy is robust. In these times, you may be able to shop around and find that dream job you have been waiting for. When the economy is doing well, employers usually have a greater demand for employees. Jobs are in abundance, and you can have your pick of numerous career opportunities found through various **online job sites** and **online job postings**. Plus, with the help of job-dedicated **search engines**, the sky is the limit.

With a booming economy, employers are more apt to open up positions or add new jobs, when they feel confident that the expense of the new employee will be offset by the profits gained. Thus, more jobs are bound to be posted in good economic times. Just knowing where to find these postings during such a time will better enable job seekers to reduce the amount of time spent on wasteful job searches. By knowing the ropes, job seekers will maximize their chances of being able to put themselves in the right place at the right time.

The Internet Has Replaced Face-to-Face Contact

Until recently, landing a job or an interview was a much more personal experience. You could get dressed in your most professional outfit and walk into a staffing agency or a private company and meet a human resources representative face-to-face. Depending on the size of the company, you could be rubbing elbows with managers, vice presidents, or the owner, depending on the particular circumstances. But in today's busy world, very rarely are such unannounced visits welcomed in the workplace. Most of the time, a job seeker who attempts to just drop in on a particular company may get no further than the receptionist.

But, with the capabilities of the Internet, everything has changed. You do not have travel from one place to the other, or schmooze your way into an office; the connections are made from the comfort of your own home, as long as you have a computer with Internet capabilities. Candidates use the Internet to submit their résumés and cover letters to potential employers. In addition, employers and staffing recruiters no longer have to conduct an initial face-to-face meeting with every job candidate; instead, employers and recruiters can choose which job candidates to bring to the next level without ever having to meet any of the initial applicants, based on information they have received in advance. Job seekers who apply for positions they are not qualified for will likely not get called in for even an initial face-to-face encounter.

In the past, a job seeker could spend several hours in a staffing agency, filling out a job application or a candidate work profile. Many job seekers were also asked to travel to an employment office where they would take numerous tests to determine their skill and proficiency levels, for such things as typing or using Microsoft® Word or Excel. A job seeker's entire day could be consumed by visits to just a few agencies.

But with the Internet, many employment agencies find most of their candidates through résumés and job applications submitted directly into their company's Web site. While some staffing agencies still require candidates to come into the office to perform various skills tests, many staffing specialists will simply send the tests to a job candidate via **e-mail**. The job seeker can open up the test through an e-mail, enter a particular code, and complete a multitude of tests — without ever leaving home. The test results are sent directly to the staffing agency, with recruiters making decisions on job candidates based on their Internet contact with a particular individual, rather than their physical contact. The technology has cut down on office traffic and made the process better in many ways for both parties, as decisions are made based on the job seeker's online materials: résumé, cover letter, and skills test results. The Internet has thus become the middleman between job seekers and employers or staffing recruiters.

Once you have applied, consider the ease the Internet offers for the rest of the job application process. If you are applying for a job in another country, you will need to know about rules, laws, and regulations for such things as entering that country. But instead of having to spend hours in the library or your local bookstore again, you can simply log on to the Internet and conduct your research. And keep in mind that you may not even

have to travel to another country for an interview abroad. While it would be nice if a particular company flew you to London for an interview, such travel is usually unnecessary with the Internet and e-mail. In fact, with the help of a program like Skype — a free software used for video conferencing and instant messaging — you may find yourself being interviewed over the computer in a virtual face-to-face setting. *Learn more about Skype and other types of virtual communication in Chapter 2.*

Internet Job Searches Offer More Variety

It has always been impractical and time-consuming to physically visit numerous companies, and many companies chose to advertise their positions strictly on a local or regional basis. Unless the position was high on the corporate organizational chart, chances were employers were not going to look farther than a 50-mile radius for qualified candidates. Few jobs were filled through a nationwide search. In many cases, the employer would hire a staffing agency to help recruit the best possible local candidate for a position.

But with the Internet, job seekers no longer have to check daily newspapers, or stumble onto positions; all they have to do is log on to the Internet to search for job postings. If he or she is interested in a particular company, the job seeker can begin by visiting the company's Web site to see what the business is about and to find out what jobs may be available anywhere in the world.

Finding jobs from coast to coast or abroad

If you are thinking about working abroad, there may be different reasons behind your decision, which may alter the way you go about your job search on the Internet. Both CareerBuilder.com and Monster.com, along with several other job sites, offer candidates the opportunity to search and apply for jobs internationally. Your dream position may be thousands of miles away — but again, thanks to technology, it may take you a mater of minutes to apply once you learn where to find the jobs and how to throw your name into the ring.

When you are pursuing a job out of state, you may want to begin looking at some of the largest companies in the country — or in the world, for that matter. A good place to research such companies is Forbes.com. In the search field, type in the names of the largest companies. Chances are, you will find a list of the top 10 and the top 100 companies. If you are looking to relocate to a different part of the Unites States, you can also check the state government job sites to find out if there are any positions that match your own experiences and skills. Of course, just wanting to work elsewhere and being able to find a position you are qualified for are two different things. Also, be sure to check each company Web site to find out if there is any type of relocation package being offered by the company you are applying for. Usually, you will find the information at the bottom of the advertisement or job posting. It will likely read something like, "Relocation expenses and fees are available for this position."

If you want to work in a museum, say in England or Istanbul, begin with research. You may first want to search the particular state or country of your choice and determine what types of jobs are available. If, in fact, you would like to find out if there are any openings at The Louvre museum in Paris, you can simply go to a search engine, such as Google or Yahoo!, and type in the words "jobs at The Louvre." Or you can search for the museum by name, and once you find the Web site, you can make your way to the jobs or career section of the museum's Web site. You may also want to take some additional time to find out what the job market is like there, along with the cost of living and the unemployment rate in case the job does not work out. You may want to begin with the U.S. Department of Labor at **www.bls.gov/ilc**. The Bureau contains a wealth of information regarding unemployment rates and employment indexes from all over the world. Whether you are interested in working in Australia, Denmark, Japan, Greece, or Spain, you will be able to find unemployment percentages, as well as whether the job market is up or down, simply by visiting the government site. You can also invest a little time in some of the government sites for the country or location you want to work in. This way, you will not find yourself strapped for cash in a foreign country. Losing a job is a stressful enough situation in your own backyard where you have learned to adapt — let alone in a country or state you just moved to.

Telecommuting or working from home is a real option

A number of jobs you can find on the Internet can be performed from the comfort of your own home. Just imagine how nice it would be to get up, have breakfast, and leisurely walk the 10 or 20 feet it takes you to get to your computer, and then sign in to a designated work site. No more traffic jams, inclement weather, colleagues to deal with — just you and your equipment.

Some caution should be exercised, though, because some of the advertised telecommuting jobs seem too good to be true — and they are. These scams boast about how easy it is for someone to make hundreds or thousands of dollars, while putting in very little time, skills, or effort. These ads usually include some type of clause whereby the job seeker must invest cash in a project, or provide an up-front payment. Do not get fooled.

By the same token, there are legitimate companies that use the Internet and do, in fact, hire people for real telecommuting positions. Good Morning America conducted an extensive study and reviewed a number of those companies, such as Alpine Access, Arise Virtual Solutions, Inc., and VIPdesk, to name a few. According to the result of the study, there are in fact jobs that you can find through the Internet, through which you can perform the work at home. They are real telecommuting opportunities. For these, you may want to visit such sites as **www.arise.com**, **www.vipdesk.com**, **www.workingsol.com**, **www.alpineaccess.com**, and **www.liveops.com**.

Some of these companies may charge a fee to get started; other companies do not charge anything. It should be pointed out that there are a number of scams that also boast about making large sums of money for very little effort. The rule of thumb is that if it sounds too good to be true, chances are, it is not real. Rather, it is just another clever method that someone has devised to free you of your money.

In contrast, Educational Testing Service (**www.ets.org**) is an example of a legitimate organization that offers at-home employment opportunities. ETS provides various types of educational testing, preparation, and assessments in addition to providing other types of educational products. ETS hires individuals who can telecommute or work from home, scoring standardized tests. According to the company's Web site, ETS develops, administers, and scores more than 50 million tests every year, providing job opportunities for a number of job seekers.

Candidates must pass the **assessments** in order to become a certified scorer. Once certified, individuals can work from home and score exams, gaining assistance from supervisors with a click of the mouse. This is just one of the many job outlets the Internet offers, allowing you to work from the comfort of your own home, but still for an outside company. If you already have a job, the telecommuting position could serve as a viable means of securing a second income, working on a part-time or limited hourly basis.

Working for an Internet company

If you are looking to work for a Web site, stop over at Google, at **www.google.com/intl/en/jobs/joininggoogle/index.html**. Job seekers are not only given a glimpse into what it is like to work for Google, but there is additional information regarding their hiring process, how to prepare your résumé or curriculum vitae (CV) specifically for Google, and tips on how to prepare for the interview. You can also read first-hand experience from Google employees. Some of the jobs include customer service positions, software engineering jobs, various technology slots, and sales positions. While some of the positions are located at company headquarters, a number of Web-based companies allow candidates to work from home. Another internet company you may want to look at is Amazon.com (**www.amazon.com**).

Producing content for an Internet company

If you are looking to see your name in print or on a Web site, there are also many opportunities to do so. While some may pay small amounts and others are done for free, it can be a good opportunity for someone who may be just out of college and needs to develop a written portfolio. There are opportunities at sites like Examiner.com (**www.examiner.com**) and About.com (**www.about.com**) where you can apply for a writing position or contribute to their sites. And, if your article is published to the Web, you may receive more compensation based on how much traffic your article generates. In addition to those types of jobs, there are still others that include writing blog posts, providing pictures, or producing other forms of multimedia for Internet users.

You have to apply for these positions like you would any other job, and usually if you are selected, you will write Web content on an area of your own personal expertise. The topics can range from fine dining to movie reviews, to crafts or current events. Most likely, you will be creating content for your company's niche, or target, market.

A Whole Different Game

Applying for a position online is vastly different than other job search activities because, for the most part, the Internet application is usually done from the comfort of your own home. You do not have to dress to impress, but you also miss out on the initial opportunity to physically meet with a potential employer or staffing recruiter to show them how truly special you are. The application process, for many entities, is paperless, and the experience impersonal.

Unlike all other job-hunting activities, the Internet may provide a job seeker with too much information about job postings, causing him or her to hesitate or be uncertain as to which jobs to spend time applying for. Through extensively using the right technology and by searching on the right sites, job seekers can narrow down the specific positions they will be applying to. Unlike job postings that appear in newspapers or other avenues, job seekers can even opt to use a specific salary range when determining which jobs to apply for and which listings to ignore. But with all of the options the Internet presents, it is easy to be overwhelmed with your job search. Thus, preparation is just as important as the search itself.

Your Must-Have List for an Internet Job Search

There are just a few items that you will need, no matter how large or small your online job search is. Use this list as your starting point for the essential, bare-bone items you must have to find your dream job through the Internet.

1) An e-mail account, complete with an e-mail address and inbox. If you have your Internet account through a cable company, chances are the company already provides such an account. If you have not done so yet, now is the time to activate your account. In the event that you do not have such an account in place, visit sites, including Google, Yahoo!, or AOL, and set up a free account. When selecting an e-mail address, remember that everything you send will carry the address. Therefore, you should avoid such names as bestbrunette@234.com, or even fastdriver@567.com or funguy@8910.com.

2) You must also have regular access to a computer, whether it is at your own home, a friend's or relative's home, or even the public library. You will obviously need the computer to create your job search materials, such as résumés and cover letters, as well as be able to access the Internet and your e-mail accounts.

3) Whether you are using your own computer or the one at the library, make sure that you have some type of word processing program that will allow you to design a résumé and cover letter. Many companies prefer Microsoft Word documents because it is the most common word processor. But, you can also use programs like OpenOffice, which can be downloaded from the Internet (**http://download. openoffice.org**) and installed on your computer for free. You may also want to have access to Adobe Reader, a program used to view, search, edit, and verify digital files. This can also be downloaded online (**www.adobe.com/downloads**), and is the software that most companies use to send and view documents, like résumés.

4) If you are using a computer other than your own, you should think about investing in a little gadget called a flash drive. You can plug it

into any USB drive in any computer and copy and store information, such as job postings, résumés, and cover letters. A flash drive works the same way as a CD-ROM or floppy disk does, but in a smaller, more convenient method. Some flash drives even come with key rings so you can attach them to your key chain, meaning you never have to worry about leaving home without it.

CHAPTER 2

Preparing for Your Online Job Search

Internet Lingo

Instant messaging: An online platform that allows people to communicate with each other instantly using their computers. It works like text messaging on a phone, where you type in your message and click a button. The recipient will receive your message immediately and can respond immediately.

Microsoft® Excel: A software program that allows the user to develop spreadsheets and create various formulas for a planned outcome. It can be used to make calculations or to organize information.

Mouse: A hand-operated device used along with a computer keyboard to carry out certain tasks and activities. It also allows a user to navigate to different locations on the Internet with a simple touch of the finger.

Real time: The present time; the here and now. When referring to communicating on the Internet, real time means to speak with someone — via computer — in present time, as you would while speaking to someone on the phone.

Skype: A software program that, when installed in a computer, allows an individual to make a call and speak to another individual, all through the use of computers. The computer actually takes the place of the telephone.

Software program(s): A program that can be downloaded or installed onto your computer to allow you to perform additional tasks that you would not be able to do without the program.

Upload: To take a document or file that has been created or stored in one computer and transfer the item to another computer, which is in a different location. An uploaded document is also known as an attachment.

Virtual face-to-face contact: The ability for two or more individuals to see each other via their computers while communicating or holding a meeting.

There will be challenges along the way because, when you use the Internet, you are probably conducting your search from home. It is easy not to get dressed, not comb your hair, and not to do any of the other things you would normally do if you were heading to a formal office setting. This is why getting in the right frame of mind is crucial for a successful job search; the Internet simply allows too much room for you to go easy on yourself. The following sections are designed to help you avoid that, and to help prepare you — physically and mentally.

Develop a Thick Skin

Rules of protocol are a thing of the past. You may not receive any word — good, bad, or indifferent — from a multitude of your job applications.

Do not take it personally, and do not get discouraged. A lack of a response may just mean there are so many applicants that the employer has found it impossible to respond to everyone who has applied. You cannot afford to get emotional about the situation.

Rejection has never come faster

In the world of online applying and hiring, rejection often comes instantly. In fact, if the company is using keyword or key phrase software, your rejection may come the day after you apply for the job. Recruiters and employers will use various methods to conduct a keyword search for potential candidates. The searches can be done through special programs, or manually. Résumés are viewed or scanned by recruiters and employers who are looking to find specific words. The words are usually standard words and phrases used in a particular industry. Most times, such words and phrases can also be found in the job advertisement as well. In addition to spotting the words, employers and recruiters may also be looking to see how the word or phrase was used and how many times it appeared in a candidate's résumé or cover letter. The "thanks, but no thanks" letter may be automated if a job candidate does not fit a particular job criterion, or if those keywords or phrases are used incorrectly or do not appear at all. Although no one likes rejection, taking a practical, rather than personal, approach to it will help you forge ahead in your job quest.

Understand that there are still going to be instances when there are other qualified candidates — or perhaps a person already working for a particular company — whom the company feels more comfortable hiring. Do not dwell on such rejection or take it personally. If you receive rejection notices, just remember that the job, for whatever reason, was not the right fit for you. Do not dwell on a rejection. Instead, move forward to the next opportunity.

If by chance you receive a rejection e-mail or letter that explains why you were not hired, you can work with the information for the next application. For example, if you are trying to get into a field where a specific skill is needed and you are told you were not hired because you did not have the particular skill, you always have the option of taking an online course to remedy the situation. If it is experience you are lacking, perhaps volunteering in your spare time will help you to get your foot in the door and gain additional experience. While the information may not help you with the original job posting, you may be able to secure the next job that comes along.

If you do receive a generic rejection, you can politely respond to the employer or recruiter and ask them why you were not selected for the position. You may inquire, in a very professional manner, what specifically made the company or agency opt for a different candidate. You are not guaranteed an answer, but it does not hurt to make the inquiry. Just remember to keep it professional. While you may have thought the position was perfect for you, the employer or recruiter was looking to find the candidate who was a better fit for their company.

If you have done your homework and you have submitted all the right tools from your cache of job search materials, there is nothing more to do but go on to the next job posting and application.

Applying for a Job is Like Having a Full-Time Job

There are times when job candidates may feel like the right job opportunity just happened to fall into their laps. However, those instances are infrequent. In most cases, a job candidate is selected only after he or she has conducted a thoughtful search, put materials together in advance, and then applied. In some cases, particularly with public or government sectors, state applications need to be filled out. These canned applications can be very time-consuming, but they are an important part of the application process.

If you are conducting a passive job search (and have all the time in the world), then you can operate at your own pace. For job seekers without this luxury, there will be a lengthy process of getting your materials organized, creating a plan, searching for a job, and finally applying for a position.

Remember that other job applicants, sometimes from all over the world, are viewing the same job listings and submitting their applications, as well. Do not put off your job search activities today, because the opportunity may not be there tomorrow. A job search can be a full-time job. Employers and recruiters cannot, and will not, wait for you. They have their own agendas, deadlines, and schedules in regard to filling positions. They usually work though the Internet with the intent of hiring someone as quickly as possible, so long as they find the right candidate. This is why job search and application should not be done as an afterthought or as a "when I get around to it" task. You may be able to apply at your own pace, but the job will more than likely need to be filled as soon as possible. Having all of your materials together will help speed up your process.

Where to Find Advice for Job Seekers

There is all kinds of career advice available on the Internet if you are willing to seek it. Advice can be found on subjects such as writing résumés, composing cover letters, acing an interview, and mastering proper etiquette for getting hired. You just need to know what is out there, what your own needs are, and where you can find advice that will best accommodate your needs.

Many of the sites mentioned in the preceding pages, like CareerBuilder. com and Monster.com, hold a wealth of information for those who do not know where to begin in terms of mapping out a career path or determining which skills are the most essential.

If you are looking for general advice, you can use Google or a niche site to type in the words, "career advice." *Learn more about niche sites in Chapter 3.* The more specific the inquiry, the better the result. For example, instead of "career advice," type in, "career advice for the recent college graduate." Click to search, and you will be amazed at the thousands of articles and columns that appear. If you typed your question into Google and clicked "Google Search," you will find numerous online articles and Web sites focused on the subject matter. Usually, the list of possible advice choices will appear in order of relevancy or popularity. The first listing may have the identical question listed somewhere in the online article, and the second listing may have similar material, but not the same identical match.

Virtual career counselors

For individuals who are not sure where to start their search or what their needs may be for landing a new job or determining if they want to stay in their field, a virtual career counselor may be perfect. In addition, a virtual career counselor may also be able to help you move to the next level in your profession, or provide advice as well as counseling if you were fired from a position and do not know what to do next.

The virtual career counselor works a little bit differently than a regular career counselor. Most times, you will physically visit a counselor's office for a help session. But a virtual career counselor may hold a session with you over the phone, or through Skype, where both parties verbally communicate with each other through their computers. This can be done via camera or video equipment attached to the computer. *Learn more about Skype later in this chapter.* There are various sites where you schedule your virtual appointment ahead of time. In some instances, the counselor may want to get a feel for your needs before the online session; therefore, you may be asked to fill out a survey or questionnaire in advance.

CASE STUDY: VIRTUAL COUNSELING OFFERS CONVENIENCE AND SOLUTIONS TO JOB SEEKERS

Dwight Bain, Coach and Counselor
The LifeWorks Group, Inc.
www.LifeWorksGroup.org
Lifeworksgroup@aol.com
407-647-7005
FAX: 407-647-8874

A place job-seekers find coaching, counseling, and guidance is the Life-Works Group, Inc., based out of Winter Park, Florida. LifeWorks Group Coach and Counselor Dwight Bain is a nationally certified counselor and life coach with some 25 years of experience.

Bain explains that there are two groups of candidates who seek out his services regularly: college or graduate students mapping out a career path, and people who have been downsized or laid off.

While standard counseling may take some time, Bain explained that counseling for job seekers moves at an alternative pace. He added that career counseling — which is designed to move job seekers from their "day jobs" to their "dream jobs" — through the Internet is a very different experience.

"It requires both the coach and client being comfortable with technology, since most contact is by telephone or e-mail," he said. "Coaching is driven by results, so it's important to see rapid progress, which keeps coaching clients motivated toward greater change."

That greater change, however, is sometimes hard to define online, Bain said. Even though the trend of virtual counseling is growing, there is a downside to it, along with other Internet-based job search activities.

"There is a great gap in relationship, so there isn't as much loyalty with online relationships as [with] face-to-face ones. And people can misrepresent or misunderstand the intended message."

Bain is also the founder of StormStress.com and served as trainer for more than 1,500 business groups. Fields and topics he is an expert in include making strategic change to overcome major stress both professionally and personally. In his years as a coach and counselor, he has seen many common mistakes made by job seekers.

"I've seen a lot of people quit their jobs out of frustration with bad managers, or even to quit out of boredom," he said. "This is a common problem since they can't wait to get out of a dead-end job, but often are in such a hurry to quit for greener pastures that they leave their day job (income) to race toward a future dream job (passion and purpose), and forget that it's a process that can take several years."

Through the long application process, it is easy to let the search get the best of you, draining you of your energy. Part of seeking the help of a counselor or a coach, Bain said, is to help the job seeker remember that a "no" is not a personal rejection; rather, it is a company simply saying the job seeker may not be the best fit.

Bain has dedicated his life to helping people achieve greater results. In addition to his work as a coach and counselor, he is a Critical Incident Stress Management expert with the Orange County Sheriff's Office. His corporate client list includes Disney, Toyota, AT&T, Harcourt, DuPont, and Bank of America. His organizational client list includes the U.S. Army, Florida Hospital, American Heart Association, the American Association of Christian Counselors, and the International Critical Incident Stress Foundation.

The
LIFEWORKS GROUP₁₋
Making Life Work for You

Things to do before the search

Before embarking on your virtual job search, it is imperative that you put yourself ahead of the game by being Internet savvy. You should be able to successfully identify the right job sites and competently prepare the type of eye-catching job tools needed to hold the attention of a potential employer.

You need to be able to know where, and how, to find valuable information that will help you grow and maximize your own skills and knowledge, in addition to being able to communicate with recruiters, employers, and others using the Internet to find qualified job candidates.

Part of being Internet-savvy is being able to perform online tasks efficiently, professionally, and quickly. Put yourself in the shoes of a potential employer — would you hire someone who was unable to compose a professional e-mail, or someone who was incapable of providing their résumé and cover letter at the time they were applying?

Also, consider the presentation of your job tools. A candidate who submits something that is unorganized or poorly put together may not be the first, or even second, choice of the employer. But if the candidate is Internet-savvy and learns how to properly format a résumé and submit it online, or how to properly write an e-mail, the outcome may be more favorable. *See Chapter 5 for more on these skills.*

CASE STUDY: SUCCESSFUL JOB CANDIDATE

Dimitry Loiseau,
San Antonio, Texas

Take the case of 19-year-old Dimitry Loiseau, a high-school graduate who secured a position in the clerical / data processing field as an Application Support Technician (AST). He presently works for the staffing agency Integrated Human Capital, where he is an AST at the San Antonio, Texas, location for Maximus. Loiseau landed his position through a job listing he found and applied for on the Internet. Loiseau has been an extremely successful job seeker using the Internet. He has found, applied, and been hired for five jobs in the last four years. All of the positions have been located through the Internet.

Loiseau not only treated his job search as a full-time, professional job, but also began by using the type of organized steps that helped him to be completely prepared for when the right job listing became available. "It was the first thing I did in the morning, and periodically throughout the day. I just started hitting the Web with all I had," he said.

Create an e-mail address and have professional tools (résumé and cover letter) ready

"I created an e-mail address that was a little more business-appropriate, like firstinitial.lastname@domain.com. Then I worked on a professional cover letter and résumé…the easiest way I found to do this was using Microsoft® Word. I borrowed a lot of my information from Microsoft templates. The way the templates word certain things is really appealing."

Visit Web sites

Loiseau visited a number of job sites daily. Some of the sites included Jobcentral.com, Snagajob.com, Sanantonio.gov, Employmentguide. com, Craigslist.org, and Monster.com. Loiseau visited a number of other sites, but found Craigslist.org to be the most effective.

Learn to be Internet-savvy

Loiseau was professional, diligent, and consistent in his job search using the Internet.

"I would consider myself a pro, or maybe even ultra-savvy, when it comes to the Internet and job search engines. I would put in at least eight applications per day on different Web sites. I applied to 30 (job listings) before acquiring the job I have now."

Handle rejections

"There were too many to count on my fingers and my toes."

Prepare for the interview

"A lot of the tips for job searches and interview advice I acquired in high school. One of my weekly exercises for my computer maintenance course was 'Professional Fridays.' We would have to dress business-professional and sit through a one-on-one interview with our instructor, where he would ask us commonly asked interview questions. It definitely made me sweat sometimes, but it gave me a good grasp on how to handle the real deal."

> **Did he find his dream job?**
>
> Probably not, he said, but it could lead him to it. Loiseau says his job has plenty of opportunities for advancement.
>
> **Advice for other job seekers**
>
> "Try to impress. Look for something you can see yourself doing for months on end. You need to make your words in your résumé, your cover letter, or anywhere else stand out as much as possible."

Set up an e-mail addresses

Having an e-mail address is crucial for the Internet job seeker, which is why this is one of the first tasks you should accomplish before starting your search. E-mail is the main form of communication for the online job application process. Yes, calls are still made to job candidates, but chances are that your first contact with a potential employer will be through e-mail. In fact, a number of job postings and company Web sites only provide an e-mail address for job candidate submissions.

E-mail is also likely to be your means for sending your résumé and cover letter to your potential employer because it is the quickest and most common form of communication. *For more information about using e-mail to send your résumé and cover letter, see Chapter 5.* Rather than having to mail out your résumé and cover letter, and waiting for days before it even reaches employers, you are able to distribute your material in a matter of seconds using e-mail.

Corresponding takes minutes, not days

The beauty of e-mail is that, with few exceptions, the message arrives almost immediately. A job posted today may not be there tomorrow, as is the case with many government jobs, which have specific times they are opened and closed to applicants. If you apply online and within the allowed time frame, your résumé and cover letter are bound to make it to the human resources department. With snail mail, however, the same may not happen.

Letter writing and sending through the postal service has decreased, with the U.S. Postal Service reporting billion-dollar losses in 2009, all as a result of the downward economy and the use of alternative communication sources, such as e-mail. In the past, not only did you have to compose a paper letter on a typewriter, but if you made a mistake while you were typing, you would have to start over from the beginning if you did not catch your mistake while composing it. Then there was the perpetual hunt for the stamp, and whether the stamp had the correct amount of postage needed to get the letter to its final destination. For all these reasons, snail mail has become a thing of the past for most job applicants. There will be certain occasions when it is a necessary vehicle — for instance, when college transcripts, or other documents that cannot be scanned, copied, or created through the Internet, are to be sent to a potential employer. For the most part, however, e-mail has become the new desired form of communication.

Job seekers can set up e-mail accounts for free on many sites, including Google and Yahoo! For example, set up a Gmail account using Google with these steps. Note that different e-mail providers may phrase their buttons and links differently:

1. Begin by navigating to the Google.com screen at **www.google. com**. At the top, you will notice various links, such as "images," "videos," "maps," and "Gmail."

2. Click on Gmail.

3. From there, you will see a screen that welcomes you to Gmail.

4. On the lower right corner, click the labeled button to create a free account.

5. Enter basic information, such as your first and last name, and your desired login name. You will be asked to create a password and choose a security question in the event that you forget your password.

6. You will also be asked to verify a word to make sure you are a person and not an automated system, and you will be asked to read and accept the terms and conditions of being a Gmail user.

7. Once you click that you accept the terms and conditions, your account will be created.

8. You will be directed to your Gmail inbox, which is where you can see new incoming messages.

9. You will have your own e-mail address, ending with @gmail.com.

10. Once you have set up your Gmail box, you can view, save, or delete e-mails when they come, and you can also compose and reply to messages.

11. Compose your message in Gmail by clicking the "Compose Mail" tab at the top left hand corner of the screen. Type the address of the person you are sending the message to in the "To" field, then enter a brief line saying what the message is about in the "Subject" line. Then, click in the large box to type the body of your e-mail.

12. If you need to attach and **upload** a document, such as your résumé or cover letter, click on the "Attach a file" link that has the paper clip next to it. A window will open that will allow you to select the location of the file you wish to upload, allowing you to choose the document you want to send. By doing this, your employer will receive the files as you created them, without having to worry about

formatting changes that can occur by just copying and pasting your résumé, for example, into the body of the e-mail.

13. To send, click "Send." Or, if you decide not to send the e-mail, click "Discard."

14. If you are not ready to send an e-mail yet, you can compose it and save it in your Drafts folder. Just write your e-mail and click "Save Now" at the top of the e-mail. Gmail also periodically automatically saves your drafts as you write them. When you are ready to send, click on "Drafts" to find the e-mail you have already written.

15. For continual access to your e-mail account, you can visit the URL **www.gmail.com**.

Say this, not that

While e-mail is less rigid when it comes to the delivery service, you still cannot forget to be professional when writing an e-mail. You may be in the comfort of your home when you are writing to a potential employer, but that does not mean that you can cut corners.

A professional e-mail should still include a formal greeting and a well-composed body, consisting of paragraphs. Do not begin your e-mail with a friendly "Hi!" Your potential employer likely does not know you, and you may come across as unprofessional and not savvy enough to fill the job opening. You should also end the e-mail in a professional manner, much like you would end a cover letter.

Also steer away from the use of slang words. Do not use anything that would indicate you are a less-than-admirable job candidate. Do not whine or tell your troubles to a potential employer, or let them know how difficult it was for you to send the e-mail. Do not ramble. The beauty of the e-mail is that it can be sent, read, and responded to, all within a matter of minutes. But if you do ramble or go off-topic, do not expect to get a reply e-mail anytime soon — or perhaps at all.

It is also wise to spell check your e-mail as you would a regular document. If you are using Gmail, you can click on the spell check function at the top right corner of your window. Many browsers automatically spell check within the text as you are typing, underlining misspellings in red. But sometimes the ease of sending an e-mail can become a problem because the usual steps, like conducting a spell check, are easy to forget when you are not using a word processor.

Smiley faces and exclamation points

While you may be reveling in all of the newfound talents you have when it comes to composing and designing e-mails, remember to keep flashiness, like colors and cute or crazy designs, to a minimum. Also avoid using things like smiley faces and exclamation points — there will be very few times when one is acceptable at all when it comes to contacting potential employers.

You will probably be thrilled to hear back from a recruiter or a potential employer regarding an application you submitted, but take a deep breath and toss on your professional hat when composing your response. Yes, it might be cute that you know how to make a winking smiley face with the semicolon and parenthesis keys ;) — but include such a comment in your e-mail and you will be looking something like this :(when the employer chooses someone more professional over you.

If you are appreciative of the offer that was extended to you in the e-mail, a much better way to phrase it would be to say, "Thank you for taking the time to speak with me."

Watching your tone

Whether you have had a hard day, or you are annoyed that no one has responded to your application, do not let it carry through to your e-mail. While e-mails are simple, they are not informal. Just because you have someone's e-mail address does not mean that you should send e-mail after e-mail regarding a particular position — or, if you find you have not been selected for a position, that you can blow off steam about an individual or the company. Simply thank them for letting you know, and move on.

If you indicate that you are a hothead through your e-mail, or a chronic complainer, what do you think your chances are of being hired? Would you want to hire someone who sent you a less-than-professional e-mail? It is doubtful.

An Even Faster Way to Communicate

Through another computer service, individuals can talk to each other through instant messaging functions, which allow people to communicate in real time. In other words, if two people in the same company want to speak with each other, but they are on different floors of the building, neither one has to visit the other; they can carry on a conversation with each other from the comfort of their own desks, and they can communicate immediately; there is no delay in the message being sent or received, thus the name **instant messaging**. Your instant messages may appear in the form of a box on your computer screen, with both your name or your user name (also known as a screenname), along with the name of the person you are communicating with. Choosing your screenname is much like choosing an e-mail address — you want something that represents you in a positive light, and also something that is easy to remember. For example, if you were applying for a public relations job, you may want to choose a screenname such as PRpro. Some job candidates match their screennames directly to

their e-mail addresses, in which case, the e-mail address for PRpro would be PRpro@234.com. Try to avoid excessive use of numbers to differentiate your name from ones that may be already taken; for instance, if PRpro is used already, try TopPRpro or YourPRpro instead of PRpro1981, as a string of numbers is not very memorable — and employers might assume the number reveals your year of birth.

As you speak to each other — by typing text in the message boxes and pressing "send" or "enter" — the complete dialogue between you and the person you are instant messaging will appear in the box. The box and dialogue will remain until you sign off or disengage in the virtual conversation. Because of the time constraints placed on both employers and job seekers, being able to correspond with each other in a matter of seconds, rather than days, makes sense. Answers — good and bad —come instantaneously.

Different providers that have instant messaging

There are a number of ways that you can access instant messaging, including AOL, MSN, Gmail's chat, and iChat, to name a few. Most of the programs can be downloaded easily. The only trick to it is that the person, or people, whom you want to be able to speak to immediately will also have to have the same program downloaded to their computer. Of course, the person must also be at their computer to receive the message and respond.

AOL: You can visit **http://dashboard.aim.com/aim** to download their free instant messaging program after agreeing to the terms and conditions. Through AIM, you can virtually connect with anyone who also has the program and talk via the computer as if you were in the same room.

MSN: You can access Windows and download a step-by-step guide to using live messenger by visiting **http://windowslive.com/Desktop/messen-**

ger. Through the instant messaging program, you can see who is online if you happen to have Hotmail and look in your Inbox.

Gmail's chat: If you have a Gmail account with **www.gmail.com** already, simply enable the Chat function at the bottom lefthand sidebar. Fellow Gmail users can chat in real time with you whenever you are both logged in to your e-mail.

iChat: You can talk to friends, see them via webcam while you are speaking, and send videos as well through your Mac computer, or even through AIM. To download the program, you can visit **www.apple.com/macosx/what-is-macosx/ichat.html**. There is also a iChat support site, which provides a tutorial as well as assistance with the program, at **www.apple.com/support/ichat**.

It should also be noted a number of the instant messaging programs and downloads are available through your cell phone, as well. You just need to find out what type of program you want, and whether it is compatible with your cell phone. A word of caution: While computer-to-computer instant messaging may be free, there may be costs associated with using the same programs with your cell phone. You may want to check with your phone carrier in advance, in order to avoid an unexpected new charge.

Skype

You can make calls through your computer through this program. As long as the person you are speaking with also has Skype, the calls — as well as instant messaging — are free. You can download the program and learn about all its capabilities by visiting **www.skype.com/intl/en/getconnected**. Unlike other instant messaging programs, with Skype, you can actually see and hear the other party through webcam and microphone. For a price, you can also subscribe to more features, such as making inexpensive calls to different countries throughout the world.

Again, if you are using instant messaging or Skype to contact a potential employer, the cardinal rule is to keep everything professional. While you may feel more relaxed using the technology from home, you should not give the impression that you are anything less than a determined, capable job candidate. This is particularly true with Skype. While a potential boss may be impressed at your ability to initiate a conference call, this is no time to skip the professional look. Nothing screams unprofessional louder than appearing on a conference call looking like you just rolled out of bed — literally. Pajama bottoms may be fine if you are only going to be viewed from the waist up, as long as you have on interview apparel from neck to waist. Ensure that your sure appearance, language, and mannerisms exhibit true professionalism.

CASE STUDY: SUCCESSFUL JOB SEEKER

Paul Milliken
Arlington, MA

Cost accountant Paul Milliken, 48, secured his position by posting his résumé on Monster.com. In fact, Monster.com was the only place the Northeastern University graduate actually posted his résumé, although he visited a number of sites, including Boston.com and Yahoo! HotJobs, during his job search. He was able to find employment in no time at all.

"I spent about two hours per day searching for a job," he said. "Monster.com was the most helpful."

To search for jobs in his area, Milliken searched for distances between his home and the job, and also the length of experience that was required for the jobs. In the end, he applied to four jobs and did not receive a single rejection during his brief search, which lasted less than a month. What he did get was a number of e-mails and calls from head hunters who found his talents, skills, and experience a hot commodity for the job market.

Preparing for All Job Possibilities

While you may have your heart set on a job at a specific company, you can use the Internet to help you prepare for all possibilities, ranging from securing a similar job to finding out what strengths you have to be successful in launching a brand new career. You can combine your intuitive skills with innovative technology for just about every job search occasion.

CHAPTER 3

The Basics of Internet Browsing

Internet Lingo

Hyperlink: A word or group of words that serves as a link to another site or subject matter. The word(s) are usually highlighted in another color and/ or underlined, and when users click on the word(s), they are rerouted to another Internet site or Web page.

Job agent: A tool or function, usually found on job sites or company Web sites, that allows the user to be sent e-mails notifying them of job openings. The job seekers fill in information about the type of jobs or job titles they are interested in. When the job or similar position becomes open, an automated e-mail is sent to the job seekers, informing them of the new opening.

Job boards: These are sites found throughout the Internet in which employers can post job listings. Job seekers can in turn visit the job boards to see what positions have been posted.

Keyword search: Typing in a specific word to conduct a search on the Internet. For example, a job seeker looking for a job as a marketing coordinator may visit a job Web site and type the words "marketing coordinator" or "marketing" to find all job listings for the position or the field of marketing.

Niche job site: A job site on the Internet dedicated to a particular industry or occupation. The site provides viewers with job postings in a specific field and usually contains job-related or industry-related information regarding that particular occupation or field.

Familiarizing Yourself With the Internet

If you have never been on the Internet, now is the time to start — particularly if you are going to find and apply for that perfect job opportunity. By using the Internet, you are able to visit various sites. If you want to begin your Internet job hunt on a basic level, start with some basic Web browsers, which will, in turn, allow you to visit other, more specific sites. These browsers may include Windows® Internet Explorer® or Mozilla Firefox®. From there, you will want to move on to a search engine, like Google or Yahoo!. In addition to those common search sites, you can also visit online newspapers, government agencies, and other locations pertaining to your job plan. Use the following steps to conduct a job search on a basic search engine:

1. Double-click on the icon of your Internet browser (Internet Explorer®, Mozilla Firefox®, Safari, or another) to open a window.

2. At the top of the window, in the location bar, type the Web address of the search engine you wish to start your search at (**www.google.com**, for example) and press the Enter or Return key on your keyboard.

3. When the Web page opens, type in your search term in the indicated box on the screen, and press Enter again.

4. After the new page has loaded, your **search results** will appear. The information will appear on numerous lines, listing **hyperlinks**, which usually appear underlined and in blue. These links begin with either an **http://** or a **www**.

5. Read the information below the hyperlinks, which usually includes brief summaries that identify information and sites compatible to your search. The hyperlinks are primarily listed in order, where the most relevant match to your search appears first, with the second more relevant listed underneath, and so on.

6. Click on the hyperlink to navigate to the page that best fits what you are searching for.

7. If you did not get the search results you were hoping for, restart your search, by starting at step 2, or by clicking on the "back" button (the arrow at the top of your browser tool bar that points to the left). Conduct a new search using more specific words and phrases — the more particular your terms are, the better your results will be.

Using your browser to get to job sites

There is a difference between a job site and search engine, although both can serve the same purpose. Search engines work by collecting information using keywords or keyword phrases. Indeed at **www.indeed.com** is a search engine that captures thousands of jobs from different sites and provides viewers with a single location for accessing the information. CareerBuilder. com lists itself as the largest job site, with more than 23 million monthly visitors. This is an example of a job site because all of the listings are job openings that are posted within CareerBuilder, and not simply gleaned from other sources on the Internet. For the purposes of your needs as a job seeker, you will be utilizing both Internet resources.

Try using your browser to visit one or more of the basic job sites or job search engines (in order to view the information this way, do not choose Craigslist for the purposes of this exercise). Once the site or search engine loads, try typing in a job title and location, and click enter again.

The job postings will also appear in the same format as the information found in your browser when you completed the steps above for your initial search. The first line of text will more than likely be the job title or the hyperlink. Underneath the link, depending on which location you chose to visit, there will usually be a brief job description. By clicking on the first line, you should be directed to the job listing. If you are on Indeed.com, you could find yourself sent to a company site, or to another search engine. By clicking on the hyperlink, you will usually be routed to the source from where the job listing originated, perhaps even in a new browser window.

In addition to providing you with details about the position, duties, and responsibilities, the posting may also include how to apply for the job. Keep looking at the job listings. Get used to seeing how they are displayed on the Internet.

Browsing for Job Listings

Whether you want to find a job with a specific company or government agency, or land a position within a five-mile radius of your home, you will first need to know how to browse online for job listings. For some sites, very general information is needed to find available positions. Search engines do the work for the job seeker by gathering job postings from numerous sources and placing them on a single location on the Internet. This way, a candidate can just go to that particular site and find multiple job listings.

In addition to knowing where the job postings are located, job seekers must also know how to get to them. Sometimes, it can be as simple as typing in a word or two, but it can also be more complex, depending on what you are searching for.

Which sites to visit first

Where to start your search will depend on your personal needs, career goals, and objectives. You may want to head straight to a niche job site, which caters to jobs in a particular field. Or, you may want to begin with a larger, more general site that serves as a search engine. The more general the **search engine**, the more job listings and perhaps extras, such as career advice or job trends, you will find.

The most popular sites and search engines collect jobs found on the Internet and compile them so they can be found in a single location. Search engines help Internet visitors by finding jobs at different locations on the Internet and making them readily available to job seekers. For instance, if you want to search for jobs as an administrative assistant or a medical technician, you would simply go to a search engine, like Indeed.com, type the job title and the location of where you want to work, and numerous job listings will come up. Some of the most widely used sites and search engines are:

- Craigslist.org (**www.craigslist.org/about/sites**)
- Indeed.com (**www.indeed.com**)
- Monster.com (**www.monster.com**)

- CareerBuilder.com (**www.careerbuilder.com**)
- Simplyhired.com (**www.simplyhired.com**)
- USAJobs.gov (**www.usajobs.gov**)
- Yahoo! Hotjobs (**http://hotjobs.yahoo.com**)

The beauty of Craigslist is that if you are looking for a job, you can view jobs in your area under occupational headings. If, by chance, you want something in the media or marketing field, simply click the link for that industry or field. Once there, you will be presented with the job postings for that area, as well as the dates the particular job advertisements were listed.

Take a little time to familiarize yourself with a few of the basic sites and search engines to get the hang of how they work. You may want to start with Monster, CareerBuilder.com, Indeed.com, or Craigslist.

Simply Hired (**www.simplyhired.com**) is a site that simplifies the process of looking for a position. All you have to do is type in a keyword or job title, along with a location. In addition to providing job postings in the United States, you can also find positions in Europe, North and South America, and the Asia/Pacific region.

Yahoo! HotJobs has become a major link to newspaper job listings. In fact, rather than just listing their advertised job postings, many newspapers have partnered with HotJobs to provide additional job information and listings through the online classified section of the newspaper. In addition to the postings, HotJobs also provides visitors with career advice and articles, as well as tools to help you apply for listings on their site.

Each site works in the same basic manner when it comes to searching for jobs. You usually enter a keyword, which could be a job title or a key phrase, along with a specific location, and click the search button. Job listings that match your search criteria will then appear. In the case of

Craigslist, there is a reversal in the basic search capability. You will click by the location first, usually a state, along with a city or town. After that, you can enter a job title in the jobs section, or just view the job postings for a particular industry or work category. Examples include administrative and office work, government jobs, and general labor.

And while the previously mentioned sites and search engines operate in a similar manner, it should be pointed out that each of them also contain attractive extras designed to increase a job seeker's ability to identify and apply for the right job, enhance their marketability, or assist in mapping out a career plan.

On Monster, you will find tools to help create profiles, as well as advice for interviewing techniques and career development, and other career-mapping and benchmarking tools. On CareerBuilder.com, you will also find advice, as well as a salary calculator, information on ways to apply for multiple positions simultaneously, skills assessments, and résumé critiques.

As for Indeed.com, the search engine provides the basics in terms of entering a key phrase or word and location, and generating numerous job postings. Other extras come in the form of being able to select job listings based on salary ranges or specific companies. In addition, Indeed.com also offers users the opportunity to join forums and discussions about positions or career-related topics.

USAJobs.gov not only includes the job search capability for finding federal government listings, but also includes a wide range of information for career plans involving the public sector. There is also a skills assessment section, as well as a brochure providing insight into government opportunities and creating online résumés.

A good place to start, regardless of the site you use, is usually at the advice section that is offered, which can usually be found under the "advice," "tools," or "Frequently Asked Questions" headings located on the top of the page on whatever site you choose to visit. The sites carry a wealth of knowledge, from topics such as leaving a position in the most professional manner, to making the most of a new job. Try some of these other popular job-hunting sites:

- Beyond.com (**www.beyond.com**)
- Dice.com (**www.dice.com**)
- Employmentguide.com (**www.employmentguide.com**)
- Hound.com (**www.hound.com**)
- ExecuNet (**www.execunet.com**) – Fee-based for executive-level search
- Jobcentral.com (**www.jobcentral.com**)
- Jobs.com (**www.jobs.com**) – Powered by Monster.com
- Jobing.com (**www.jobing.com**)
- Juju.com (**www.job-search-engine.com**)
- Snagajob.com (**www.snagajob.com**)

Niche Sites and Job Boards for Specific Occupations and Industries

You may want to start with your local newspaper's search engine to find out whether they have a Web site and, if so, how their classified section is presented.

There are also industry-specific job sites and **job boards**, which are Internet locations that allow employers to post job openings that deal with positions in a specific field, industry, or for a particular occupation. One interesting site is Beyond.com (**www.beyond.com**), which allows users to go to the site and to search other niche sites within the site. While Beyond. com bills itself as the largest network for niche job sites, there are many other sites tailored to a particular industry or occupation. For example, JournalismJobs.com (**www.journalismjobs.com**) provides leads and job postings related to the field of journalism. The site also offers users an opportunity to create an online job-seeker folder in addition to providing a cache of other resources designed to help journalists find and secure a position in the field.

Some of these other niche sites include:

- Accounting.com (**www.accounting.com**) – For jobs in the field of accounting

- Administrativejobsite.com (**www.administrativejobsite.com**) – For positions in the administrative and clerical field

- Autojobs.com (**www.autojobs.com**) – For positions in the field of auto mechanics

- Bankjobs.com (**www.bankjobs.com**) – For jobs dealing with the banking and financial industry

- Biotech (**www.biotech.com**) – For positions in the field of biotechnology

- Idealist.org (**www.idealist.org**) – For positions and volunteer opportunities in non-profit groups as well as other institutes and organizations

- JournalismJobs.com (**www.journalismjobs.com**) – For positions in the field of journalism, as well as publishing and writing

- Marketingjobs.com (**www.marketingjobs.com**) – For jobs specifically in the field of marketing

- Medzilla.com (**www.medzilla.com**) – For positions in the health care industry
- Nonprofitjobs.org (**www.nonprofitjobs.org**) – For jobs with nonprofit organizations
- Talentzoo.com (**www.talentzoo.com**) – For jobs in the marketing and advertising field

 Job Tip!

If you Join CareerBuilder.com and apply for positions through the Web site, you will be e-mailed periodic job recommendations that list numerous jobs that have been posted and match your own criteria, to some degree.

Helpful sites for job seekers dealing with diverse situations

There are numerous sites tailored to accommodate just about every job seeker's circumstances. Whether you are an older worker, or a student who just graduated from college, there are specific sites designed especially for you. These sites carry information regarding the types of problems you may be faced with. There are also a number of diversity sites tailored for specific job seekers based on ethnicity or other related categories. Some of those sites include:

- LatPro.com (**www.latpro.com**) – A job board for Hispanic and bilingual job seekers

- Diversityworking.com (**www.diversityworking.com**) – A site that carries a variety of positions geared toward different genres

- IMDiversity.com (**www.imdiversity.com**) – Includes all kinds of advice for minorities in addition to diversity jobs

Government Job Sites

Job applicants are not the only ones taking to the informational highway. As a result of the Internet's advantages as a viable and practical employment tool, many government entities are also turning to the Internet as their primary means of locating job candidates.

If you are looking to find a job with the federal government, then **www. USAJobs.gov** should be your first stop. As the official job site of the federal government, the site has joined other job search engines and forums in providing visitors with a vast array of advice, including information about how to apply for government jobs. The Web site has come a long way, as the method for filling government jobs of the past is explained on the home page. *For a list of resources for state government jobs, see Appendix B.*

If you visit Recovery.gov (**www.recovery.gov**) and click on the top of the page under "opportunities," you will find another link for recovery-related jobs. The link will direct you to the federal job site, USAJobs.gov. From there, you can head to the classification titled American Recovery and Reinvestment Act (ARRA) Jobs, which will allow you to search for newly created jobs in your area.

In addition to listing job openings, USAJobs.gov — which is run by the United States Office of Personnel — provides more to its users. There are sections dedicated to assisting veterans with the employment application process, as well as advice to help active-duty service men and women transition into the private sector's work environment. There are sections dedicated to helping users understand federal processes and terminology, as well as other parts dedicated to helping would-be applicants learn the latest information about federal hiring trends.

Local and state government job listings can usually be found on municipal Web sites, such as USA.gov (**http://www.usa.gov/Agencies/State_and_ Territories.shtml**).

Certain positions may also be located through some of the bigger search engines or niche sites, as well. For example, if you are looking for a position as a Chief Executive Officer (CEO), you may want to begin your Internet journey at **www.Execunet.com**, which is an online membership site catering to senior-level executives who are used to working in jobs that carry a six-digit salary range.

Many of the government job postings include dates indicating when the position was opened, and applicants can begin applying for the position. The dates when the posting will be closed, meaning no additional applicants will be considered, can also be found. There is usually information regarding who can apply for the job, the minimal standards (like U.S. citizenship), and whether special consideration will be given to a particular job candidate classification, such as military veterans or retired federal government employees.

Special Functions of Job Sites

Now that you have an idea of which sites have the best features and functions for your job search, the trick is to decide which sites make the most efficient use of your time, and how you are going to develop a personalized plan for your job search. Different sites offer different features, from creating a personalized account that saves your information to using the Web site to help you apply to a mass of jobs at once. These special functions are designed to make your job search a little easier.

Storing your information for fast applications

A number of sites will also store your information once you have registered with them and created a profile. After you fill out an initial job application with information, including your name, address, e-mail address, and phone numbers, then you move on to submitting your résumé. If you complete the application once, you will be able to apply for a number of other job positions in the future simply by filling out your name and your e-mail address.

For example, once you are registered with sites like CareerBuilder.com, Monster.com, and SnagAJob.com — which can be done at no cost to the job seeker — your information for the specific job you want to apply for, as well as any other jobs that may come your way, will be kept in your own online file. It should be noted that several other job sites do charge a fee to register or for regular membership. Be sure to read everything beforehand.

To begin with a site like CareerBuilder, visit **www.careerbuilder.com**:

1) Click on "Sign in," or the "My CareerBuilder" tab to direct you to the page where you can sign up for an account.

2) You will be given the option of signing in (if you are already a member) or registering as a member.

3) As a new user, you will be asked to complete a page of information, including creating your online user name, creating a password, and providing contact information about yourself, such as your e-mail address, physical address, phone number, and whether you are a job seeker or a potential employer.

4) Once you have filled in all of the required information — which should take no longer than a few minutes — you can go to the bottom of the page and click "Register Now."

5) From there, you will be sent a welcome e-mail from the site, thanking you for joining.

6) Once you are a registered member, you can continue using the site to post your résumé and build a professional Internet presence. *See more about building this presence in Chapter 8.*

Sites that help you apply to multiple jobs

Some sites like CareerBuilder.com will lead you to another page with similar job listings once you have applied for a job. On CareerBuilder.com, for example, you find an administrative assistant's position you want to apply for. You may be sent to another screen confirming that your application was successfully submitted. In addition, you will also find a box with numerous job listings (depending on how many postings there are for that particular job), on the same page. The box may contain many jobs that say "administrative assistant," as well as "executive administrative assistant," or "administrative specialist." There will be a message that states any of the job listings with an empty box in front of them can be applied for.

You can check one or all of the boxes, and the box at the bottom or the top of the page, which says "Quick Apply Now." If you have registered with the site, then you can take advantage of the job tool. If, for example, there are nine new jobs you want to apply to, and you checked the boxes beside each job title, then once you click quick apply now, your résumé is e-blasted, or sent all at once, through the Internet and into the human resources departments for each of the nine different companies which you wanted to apply to. You can blast your résumé to multiple employers with a single click.

Another such site that allows you to blast your résumé to numerous sites is RésuméRabbit.com (**www.resumerabbit.com**). According to the site, if you choose to send your résumé, it will be submitted to nearly 90 job-dedicated sites, job banks, and search engines. In addition, users will receive reports letting them know which sites their résumés are now posted to. Employers can then browse your résumé and cover letter when they log onto these sites. E-mailed job matches — consisting of job listings that match your profile or criteria — will also follow.

Again, while a number of these little features are available for free, there are some sites like RésuméRabbit.com that may involve a fee of slightly less than $60. The site also indicates that through them, your résumé can be sent to up to 87 sites, with little time and effort on your part. Be sure to read everything on a site before you send out multiple résumés, though. The goal of these functions, whether you use the ones offered for free or you pay a fee, is to send and post your résumé to as many Internet venues as possible, increasing the likelihood that a potential employer will see your résumé.

Sites that inform you when new jobs have been posted

You can also set up **job agents** for yourself. A job agent is a tool that allows you to sign up for e-mail notifications for job openings based on your preferences and job search criteria. By filling out information about the type of jobs you are interested in, the site sets up an automatic alert for when those jobs become available and e-mails you.

Some sites, like GetEditingJobs.com (**www.geteditingjobs.com**), allow you to have these job agent updates sent to your e-mail daily or weekly. In those updates, the job seeker is given a list of critical jobs that employers are looking to have filled as soon as possible, in addition to a link for standard job listings.

For example, if you are looking for a position as a legal secretary in Atlanta, all you have to do is set up a job search agent and indicate the type of position you are looking for, and the location. When legal secretary jobs in the Atlanta area become available or are posted somewhere on the Internet, you will receive an e-mail telling you about the job opportunity. The e-mail will also contain a link, directing you to the job posting. You can click the link and be sent directly to the job posting or, in the case of Indeed.com, you may be sent to the Web site where the posting originated from. You can apply from there.

You even have the opportunity to set up multiple job agents. If, for example, you are looking for a job that puts your writing skills to use, one job agent could alert you to the new writer's positions in your job search proximity. A second job agent could alert you to all newly posted freelance writing positions. A third job alert could be set up to inform you about all of the new jobs in the communications field, which have been freshly entered into the Internet. Once the job agent has been created by you, e-mails will arrive about new positions as they are posted online. You can review the opportunities and decide whether you want to apply to any (or all) of the new job listings.

Sites that localize your search

Some sites, like Jobing.com (**www.jobing.com**), allow users to take a localized approach to their job search. Candidates can begin their search by entering a particular zip code. They will be directed to another screen, where they can type in a job title or word. In addition to job listings, the site also features articles and information on specific local employers with jobs. The site also covers information about upcoming job and career fairs. There is also a section listing various local community job blogs, based on the zip code you originally entered.

CASE STUDY: SUCCESSFUL JOB-SEEKER

Danielle Constantakes,
Marietta, GA

Sometimes, being at the right place and time when it comes to finding a job through the Internet does pay off — if you are willing to put in the work and the effort.

Take, for example, the case of Danielle Constantakes, of Marietta, Georgia. She was able to use the Internet to land a position in the accounts payable division of a corporate accounting department.

Constantakes, up until recently, had found and secured all her prior positions through traditional means, not using the Internet. She was able to go into a company and fill out an application; or, through word-of-mouth, she learned of work opportunities that she subsequently applied for and was hired for.

While she did have a support and network base in another state, the Internet became her primary lifeline to job opportunities once she relocated to Georgia.

With few people to depend on, and having little-to-no experience with the companies in her new community of residence, she turned to the Internet as a means to find and secure a position in her field of accounting.

"My day would start in front of the computer where I would visit sites including Monster.com, Careerbuilder.com, Jobs.com, and Craigslist.org," she said. "From there, I would also visit some of the smaller job sites and the local newspaper sites."

Constantakes said that she spent at least two hours a day combing through the job listings and new postings. "I would start with the most popular job sites and begin by using a **keyword search** and typing in 'accounts payable' or 'accounting' to find job listings.

Once she found positions in her field that she was qualified for, Constantakes said she spent the rest of the time customizing and tailoring her tools to fit the position she was applying for.

> While it may have been difficult at times, Constantakes said she was able to successfully find and get hired for a position she liked that was in her field of accounting expertise.

Search engines that direct you to new job opportunities

There are also search engines that will capture many jobs from different job boards. If you type in a job title and a location, these engines, such as Indeed.com, will often come back with hundreds of jobs that matched your word search criteria.

For example, if you type in the job title "medical assistant," you may be presented with 200 job positions, giving you even more options. This happens because the results have not only turned up all the jobs that have the title "medical assistant," but the search included much more: The search engine might have also returned additional job listings that had one or both of the words "medical" or "assistant." There may be additional opportunities for you in the medical profession that do not have to do with being an assistant. When this occurs, the job site is directing you to new opportunities you may have otherwise never applied to. Keep in mind, however, that not all search results will match your personal criteria.

In some instances, you may find yourself applying for a job that is no longer available. On sites like Beyond.com, if you click on a particular job title and find the position is no longer available, you will be provided with a list of other jobs that closely match your job search criteria. These postings may include a wide variety of job titles, but usually include the essential duties and responsibilities of the job you originally wanted to apply for.

Other sites, like CareerBuilder.com, will e-mail you job recommendations, including a list of jobs that match some of your own profile criteria. In addition to letting you know the job title and location of the hiring company, the e-mail may also contain information on how popular a particular job is, based on the number of applicants who have applied using the particular Web site.

You will find unique functions, like these, helpful during the course of your online job search, as they serve to make jobs more accessible and the task of applying a little less time-consuming. But, before you are ready to apply for jobs and take advantage of these special features, you need to get organized for your job search.

CHAPTER 4

Getting Organized For Your Internet Job Search

Internet Lingo

Assessments: A means to measure your proficiency level for a particular skill or your knowledge for a specific program or topic, using standardized methods. The assessments can be written or verbal. Both types can be done online.

Blog: A Web site where an individual can make daily or weekly entries for others to read.

Chronic job applicant: A person who continually applies to one job after another. The applicant may or may not be qualified for the positions they apply to, they may not do research on companies they are submitting their applications to, and they may forgo the essentials, such as including a cover letter. They apply to positions daily, weekly, or monthly, usually without achieving success.

Job campaign: A series of events and actions taken by a job candidate to achieve their mission of securing a job.

Skills test: A means to measure your knowledge of a particular subject, or a particular topic, craft, or program.

Tutorial: An online instructional manual that can be found under the help section of most computer programs or applications.

Applying to jobs online without a plan is like threading a needle with your eyes closed. You may get it eventually, but how much time have you wasted in the process?

Without forethought and planning, you can find yourself aimlessly applying to jobs, hoping — rather than expecting — to be called, interviewed, and hired. This type of blind job-searching behavior can be called chronic, and is something a successful job-seeker aims to avoid.

Organization is also essential if you are going to conduct a job search that will lead to landing a job. Keeping all of your materials in a central location and being able to access the items quickly will go a long way when it comes to applying online; therefore, organization is key.

How To Avoid Becoming A Chronic Job Applicant

Because of the ease in finding jobs, and the amount of time a weak job search entails, individuals can find themselves applying over and over to jobs, even though their applications yield few or no results. Through the Internet and certain sites, job seekers can find a job, enter only a bit of personal information, and apply for a position in a matter of seconds. Applying to random jobs is not enough, though, and often makes you a **chronic job applicant**.

If you were getting up each morning and visiting each company you were applying to, the list would be vastly scaled down because of the travel, the amount of time you would have to spend at each location, and the business hours the particular company operated under. But you are not bound by any of those restrictions when applying through the Internet. All you have to do, in most circumstances, is click, click, click. The simplicity is a double-edged sword, especially for individuals who do not want to do any advance work.

 ## Job Tip!

Some companies or government agencies will limit the number of positions you may apply to, or limit the period of time in which you can apply for a position. Take care when applying because you may face a waiting period if your dream job happens to open up and you have already applied for another position at the same company. The circumstances differ from company to company.

Being a chronic job applicant can take its toll on a job seeker in many forms, like in a loss of confidence. It will cause the job seeker to merely go through the motions of applying for jobs, preventing him or her from distinguishing which company or staffing agency is interested or has already rejected him or her. It certainly will not help your morale when you apply over and over and get no response, or just rejections. Eventually, the situation will leave you feeling as if you cannot get a job if your life depended on it. It may cause a knee-jerk reaction in which you start redesigning all of your tools, such as your résumés and cover letters. In your haste to rectify the situation, you may not stop to make sure you conducted a proper spell check.

By taking a fly-by-the-seat-of-your-pants attitude to the job search, you could be missing out on extraordinary opportunities. For example, if you apply to all the jobs listed under "communications assistant" without taking the time to assess your skills and evaluate your experience, you may actually be qualified for a higher position without even knowing it. You could be limiting yourself and missing key areas where your own stock would be greatly valued.

Furthermore, if you are rejected once at a certain company but have been conducting a massive and general job search, the chances that you will apply to the same company again — accidentally — are high.

Your chances of becoming burnt-out are not the only thing that this chronic application behavior can affect. Consider your self-esteem. The more places you apply to randomly, without necessarily having the qualifications necessary for those particular positions, the more open you leave yourself to rejection. Imagine working on a project day in and day out, only to have your work, rejected over and over. Your confidence and self-esteem are likely to take a direct hit, and the Internet can be a cruel tool when it comes to getting an impersonal rejection. There is no one to ask why you were not the right fit, or if it was something in your materials that led them to another candidate. Rejection, in general, is not something you want to go out of your way for, but that is exactly what you can subject yourself to by chronically applying to jobs.

Deciding on Your Options, Goals, and Mission

Deciding on your options, goals, and mission will go a long way in avoiding some of the pitfalls of chronically applying for jobs. You may want to ask yourself what your options are for other jobs. Whether you want to stay in your own field, want to try something different, or are qualified for something different are all factors to take into consideration.

Your mission defines what is important to you; it is what you want to achieve through your job search activities and actions. You may wish to consider the following when defining your mission:

1. *Location:* Narrow the job search down to a particular zip code or within a certain range of a city; try **www.snagajob.com**.

2. *Salary:* Begin with a particular job posting and then narrow down your choices by salary range; try **www.indeed.com**.

3. *Long-term goals:* Ask yourself if the position you are applying for fits your long-term goals. You may want to begin by visiting a larger Web site, such as **www.monster.com**, which can also provide tools to help you map out a path from a present position to an end career goal.

Mission: To be hired as a communications coordinator in a large firm, within a 20-mile radius of my home.

Under the mission of the communications coordinator example, you will need to set up your goals — the means to accomplish your mission. Your goals for your Internet job search could include:

1. Search for communications coordinator positions through various job sites and search engines using the specific title. You can tailor the search to include jobs in a certain location (which is located no further than a 20-mile from your home).

2. Identify the large companies within the 20-mile radius of your home.

3. Browse the large company Web sites to determine if there are possible openings for a communications coordinator.

4. If a position or positions are found, conduct research on the companies to determine if they are good matches for you, and they fit your own mission.

5. Review and act on any additional options that you may have uncovered through your job search.

For example, there is a communications director posting for one company, and a communications specialist position in a second company. Each job may present a potential opportunity for you. They may not be exactly what you started out looking for, but each one may hold new possibilities. The communications specialist position may help you get your foot through the door, but the communications director posting is a higher position than you had envisioned for yourself. Be flexible and willing to review and act on all options. You may include a variation of the mission statement as your objective, but it may not be the exact same statement. In the case of the above example, your résumé objective may read something like: "To secure a communications position in a company that allows me to utilize my skills and talents to achieve success by further enhancing the company's corporate image." The two statements are very different: One is important to your needs, and the other is important to a company's needs.

Having a clear mission or objective statement is better when it is fine-tuned to say something specific. It should be pointed out that the mission is not exactly the same as the objective, which may be placed on your résumé. Once you have established what your mission or objective is, then you can plan your goals as a means to accomplish your mission. You can structure the goals in a way to include the specific tasks that need to be completed and the deadlines in which the tasks have to be performed.

Other criteria to use for goal-setting

It might be wise to begin by jotting down the specific type of job(s) you are searching for, now that you have fine-tuned your mission and objective. You may also want to list any types of criteria "musts" that you will look for in a job advertisement before you apply. These may be similar to the aspects you considered for your missions statement.

From there, you may also want to think about the next level of criteria you would like your job to meet, but that are not deal breakers — these are your wants, not needs. Say, for example, you are looking to get into the theater as a backstage worker. You may want a certain level of pay; however, you see a job that is a perfect match that pays less than your ideal amount. You may decide to compromise on the pay in order to get your foot through the stage door, because getting involved in the industry is a more important criterion than the pay.

Once you have identified your own needs and wants, you should decide how much time you will be spending on your job search. You should also take into consideration that the process will not only include visiting Web sites, but applying for positions as well.

Tips to Maximize the Time Spend on Your Job Search

Never underestimate the value of a strategy. While some people can take on their tasks spontaneously and have everything come out perfectly, the same cannot be said for most individuals. Having a good strategy — which includes identifying where you are today, where you want to be, and the steps you need to take to get there — is the type of organization that helps you overcome obstacles along the way.

Do your homework

Say you want to work as a Web developer and, while you have had some informal experience through your previous position, you do not have formal training in Web development. You would want to do your research on what is required of a Web developer by reading job postings to get a sense of what skills are necessary and seem to be repeated in all the postings you read. You would also want to research Web development itself to be up-to-speed on the latest trends, challenges, and future job projections.

Once you have collected the necessary information, you must map out a plan to be able to compete with fellow job seekers. You may need to take additional courses online, or you may need to speak with a virtual career counselor if you were let go from your last position and cannot receive a reference about your previous work. You may also want to research related fields and positions that you may be qualified for and that will help you to eventually land a Web developer's position.

Ultimately, identifying these actions and taking all of these steps comprises your strategy, which is the course to move you from where you are today to where you want to be in the future.

Set a schedule for yourself

Most people use a schedule to get things done. Remember, it was much easier planning your day when you knew where you would be from 8 a.m. to 5 p.m. — at work. If your boss allowed you to come in when you felt like it and do the work when you were up to it, this would probably not be very productive for the company.

Thus, if you are going to be successful, you need to make a schedule to keep yourself on track. Let us say that you are conducting a daily search and treating the process as a full-time job. You may want to make a schedule that includes responding to professional e-mails from 8 to 9 a.m., with job search slated for 9 to 11 a.m., listing top choices as you go along, and keeping track of the job agents you sign up for. After lunch, the rest of the day may include spending from 1 to 3 p.m. altering both your résumé and cover letter to make them specific to the jobs you will be applying for. The time slot from 3 to 5 p.m. will be spent actually applying for jobs. You may also want to take a few minutes, say from 5 to 5:15 p.m., to create a list or schedule for tomorrow's tasks.

This type of schedule will go far in helping you to reach goals and accomplish your mission of securing a new job. A schedule that includes searching and applying for positions in between movies or TV shows will not be nearly as productive. Job search is your new job — not just when you can squeeze it in, while being involved in other activities.

CASE STUDY: SUCCESSFUL JOB SEEKER

Susan Newell
Marietta, GA

"In total, I must have applied to over 200 positions throughout my job search and work career, resulting in employment at four different jobs. None of this, however, would have been possible without the Internet.

I started to look for jobs online, visiting sites like CareerBuilder, Yahoo HotJobs, Monster, and the Web sites for staffing agencies, and sent out lots of résumés. I would start every morning, looking to see what new listings of jobs there were.

In order to find a job and to increase my chances of getting hired, I included key phrases and words from the job advertisements I applied to. Some of the items included such terms as year-end adjustments, W-4's, COBRA, tax questions and policies, garnishments, and various computer programs as well. I was also familiar with the phrases that were common to the industry. I took the key points I found in the job postings and incorporated them into my résumés and my cover letters.

While the phrases may not have meant much to everyone, I knew that they would mean something to the recruiter or human resources representative who would be reviewing my résumé. I also spent a lot of time searching for job postings that matched my own skills and experiences.

This was an important part of the job search process for me because even though I did have the experience, it allowed me to stay up-to-date with the work issues and responsibilities that were very important to employers who were hiring people in my field.

Through the Internet, I was able to secure a position processing payroll for a national payroll company, which was in my own field of payroll. Prior to my job search, I was pretty familiar with the Internet, and pretty skilled in terms of knowing how to use it for my job search and being able to create my résumés and cover letters."

Keep your tools on hand

When you apply for more than one job, it helps to have all of your pertinent information handy on the computer. You may be asked to provide names, addresses, e-mail addresses, and phone numbers of your references on each application, in addition to providing your résumé. You may also be asked about any awards or certifications you may have. It will make things easier when all of this information is arranged in a location that is easy to access.

Rather than going back and finding contact information, or the months, dates, and years you were working at a specific location, having the information at your fingertips at all times will be a tremendous time saver. This is particularly true when applying for government positions, where they want as much detail as possible.

Create a computer folder for cover letters, résumés, and portfolios

Having a folder on your computer containing cover letters, résumés, and portfolios is another way that you can always be ready when the perfect job opportunity presents itself, therefore saving yourself tremendous amounts of time with each application. There is nothing more time-consuming than rewriting these materials or compiling these materials over and over again. *For information on how to create a digital folder for storing your application tools, see Chapter Five.*

From a purely practical approach, it makes sense. If you are thinking in terms of having a hard copy of your job tools, you certainly would not redo your résumé and cover letter from start to finish if you were applying for several jobs; chances are, you would just make copies of the documents and send them out. With the Internet, the task is even simpler, and you will be able to tailor each cover letter and résumé to fit any job type with just a few tricks of cutting and pasting.

Keep up with job market news and industry changes

It does not hurt to keep up with the news regarding a particular job market, such as the market in a particular location. Keep in mind that job market trends are important: It may not be the best time to apply for a particular job when you see that thousands are being laid off during a particular week. Also, if you are looking for answers regarding a particular question about the pay range for a job in a specific location, there are certain sites that have a large category of insightful articles.

Learning about changes in an industry and being able to talk about those changes could mean the difference in landing the job — or having the employer choose someone else who is more on top of the trends. Sites to find such news include:

- Forbes.com (**www.forbes.com**) – Provides a wealth of business and industry insight and knowledge. You can go to the search box at the top of the page and type in the particular industry you are looking at, such as biotechnology or finance. Once you click "Search," the Web site will bring up a large selection of information — in the form of articles — regarding that particular industry.

- Yahoo.com, under biz.yahoo (**http://biz.yahoo.com**) – Offers newsworthy information relative to businesses and industries.

- MSN.com (**www.msn.com**) – Carries the top events of the day with very up-to-date information regarding finances and stock market news.

- Another valuable site is the U.S. Department of Labor (**www.dol. gov**). You can find all kinds of data regarding industry trends, as well as job growth and projected growth for the coming years.

How has the job changed?

You need to know a little history about the position you are vying for in order to truly appreciate the trends occurring in the job market for the position you are applying to. For instance, if you are applying to be a sales representative for an upscale store, you should know that the job used to entail meeting with customers and encouraging them to make new purchases. As long as the foot traffic came through the door, the sales representative would have a fair to good opportunity to make the sale. However, that may have been the way daily business was run 15 or 20 years ago.

 Job Tip!

Review sites and online articles to learn specific information on what types of experience and credentials are needed to get you to the next level of your career path.

The sales representative you strive to be will have the same merchandise from ten years ago when the selling process was done by traditional methods, and may still be dealing with customers — but now in a virtual world. Rather than face-to-face contact, the sales rep may use the Internet, so instead of being able to walk customers to a product for a first-hand, the sales rep might have to make a more graphic, verbal pitch in order to land the sale. Customers may be buying from Web sites and virtual catalogues where there is no touching or personal view of the product before the purchase.

Thus, the sales rep may now be seated in front of a desk and computer, rather than standing in front of a cash register. While the product itself may not have changed, the environment and the types of skills necessary to be a sales representative in a successful sales venue have. The product may be sold exclusively through the Internet. In addition to knowing how to process an online order, the sales rep may now have to wear a headset to answer calls from customers. Additionally, he or she may have to learn new computer programs that act as the company's purchase- or customer-mailing database.

Remember to research the changes in the industry and use technology to stay on top of the changes. Although selling products as the sales rep, for example, will still be your ultimate task, being knowledgeable about how methods of doing this task have changed will improve your chances of getting, or staying, employed in your field.

Take Stock of Yourself

Another crucial step in organizing your job search is to take a hard, honest look at yourself. A good way to take stock of yourself is to get to know yourself; as William Shakespeare once wrote, "To thine own self be true." The advice, although written centuries ago, is still timely. In order for you to procure a job, you must know yourself — including your strengths and weaknesses.

Thanks to the Internet, you can evaluate yourself, thus helping you to pinpoint the skills you excel at, while also learning about your personal work style. These types of evaluations have been done through various other avenues, but the Internet has just made the process that much easier, and relatively painless. The assessments come in many forms, from self-testing to analysis and online virtual counseling.

The way that the tests are written may help to uncover skills that you did not even know you had. Some tests are designed to determine your character, personality, or work skills, while others help recommend job industries and professions that you may be able to flourish in based on your assessment test results. Once you have taken the test, the results are usually immediately available. The assessments — which can range from assessing your typing skills to your proficiency in a particular computer program or application — may be free or at-cost.

Take, for example, the assessment offered by JobDiagnosis.com. Job candidates can go to the Web site (**www.jobdiagnosis.com/registration. htm#back**) and fill out a registration form, complete a short survey, and receive a complimentary job diagnosis, which will provide a brief analysis on the industry and job type you are suited for, based on your survey answers.

Put yourself to the test

The credentials on a job seeker's résumé are no longer just the calling card or preview of coming attractions. Job candidates vying for some positions should expect to be tested on any of the skills they say they have. A graphic designer, for example, may not only have to provide proof of past work, but may also be expected to show — through testing — their knowledge of programs such as InDesign, Photoshop, or DreamWeaver.

For individuals who will be using computer skills and various programs, do not be surprised if you go to fill out an application and find the company has scheduled you to take computer program skills assessment tests online prior to being called in for an interview. Such testing does not occur for all jobs, but be prepared before you apply. Do not overstate your experiences or proficiency levels, because you may be asked to prove it. A very popular site for companies who test their candidate's is Kenexa Prove It (**www. proveit.com**), which offers over 1,000 assessment tests.

Regardless of your situation, begin with the basics. If you are searching for any type of office position, chances are that you will be asked to take several assessment tests to see how qualified you are for a position. The tests are standardized, although different companies and agencies use different variations. For instance, if you are asked to take an assessment test to determine your proficiency level using Microsoft® Word, you could end up with a very basic, general test, in which your ability to navigate through Word is assessed. You may be asked the steps for creating labels for a mail merge, or how to change a document from portrait to landscape setup, or even how to conduct a simple spell check of a document. You may find yourself taking a more advanced proficiency test for the same program, depending on the skills the company requires you to have.

While you may have known how to use the entire suite of Microsoft® Office programs inside and out several years ago, there may have been changes and updates you are not familiar with. Or, you may have only been asked to use certain parts of the program in your most recent jobs, and you have become somewhat rusty on other aspects. Some tests will recognize shortcuts that you can take to achieve a certain task, while other tests may only be designed to recognize the formal way a task should be carried out in a particular program.

Likewise, there are sites to assess other specific skills. If you want a quick assessment of your typing skills, visit Typingtest.com (**www.typingtest. com**). The site allows visitors to take a free one-minute typing test. The site also includes information on receiving various typing certificates.

Other job sites also include some form of assessment tests, designed to test everything from your negotiating skills to your coping skills to your potential for a new career. You can visit them at:

- **www.hotjobs.yahoo.com/assessment**
- **www.queendom.com/tests/testscontrol.htm?s=71**
- **www.livecareer.com**

It is particularly important to have an accurate assessment of your computer and program skills because you may be asked to take similar tests by a potential employer. If you are asked to rate yourself as highly proficient in a particular computer program, be prepared to take an advanced test on the subject, rather than a basic test. Tests, depending on the type of test and where it is offered, vary from multiple-choice to task-oriented, but use the following as a sample of the types of questions you may be asked.

Sample Skills Computer Test
1) What steps do you take to create a document?
2) How do you change the text from regular to bold in a document?
3) Show how you would cut and paste specific text.
4) Draw a table with five columns and ten rows.
5) Insert a clip art picture Into a document.
6) Underline this question.
7) Change the font type from Arial to Calibri.
8) Change the view of a document from normal to print view.
9) Open a worksheet up in Excel.
10) Show how to arrange the data in a column using the ascending sign.

Basic Math and English Skills Test
1) (7 x 4) + 698 =
2) (5/10) X (6/8) =
3) You received 20 boxes this morning. If you give one department three boxes, and two other departments give you nine more boxes each, how many boxes do you have at the end of the day?
4) 1,357; 2,468; 3,579; what is the next group of numbers that should follow?
5) Your late again. (What is the error in the sentence?)
6) Give me Janes' coat. (What is wrong with the sentence?)
7) I am going to dress up as a which on Halloween. (What is wrong with this sentence?)

Job Tip!

If you find that you need to brush up on your skills, use reference sheets by Quickstudy.com (**www.quickstudy.com**). The company makes laminated instructional guides for all kinds of subjects, like Microsoft® Word, Excel, and PowerPoint, as well as grammar, math, and punctuation.

Online courses to brush up your skills

What happens when you do not perform as well as you thought you would on your skills assessment tests? As a low-cost, initial solution, you may want to spend a little time going over a program **tutorial** to strengthen the areas that the test identified as weak. Many of the computer programs will come with their own tutorials, or you may want to visit Web sites, such as Microsoft.com, to search for a tutorial that will help you renew your knowledge of an application and the ways in which tasks are carried out.

If you need to strengthen your skills in an area that is not related to a specific program, but rather to the duties of a particular job, there are online courses available, too. Rather than having to wait for a particular course to be offered at a certain location, many online resources are available to you whenever you choose to take advantage of them. Self-help courses and tutorials can be done any time with certain types of courses that are available 24 hours a day, seven days a week.

Taking advantage of all of these avenues for assistance can only improve your chances of conducting a successful job search. If you want to apply for a particular position and are lacking a key type of training, skill, or trait mandatory for the job, then the Internet can be your tool to achieve success — but only if you are organized in the way you conduct your search.

 Job Tip!

Many skills assessments are free and, in some cases, job seekers can get results designed to help match them to a position or industry based on their personality traits.

What types of skills can you increase online?

Whether you are hoping to become a teacher, a personal trainer, Web developer, or a hotel concierge, chances are you will be able to find an online course that will help you to perfect your skills. You can begin by conducting a search regarding the credentials and online courses you will need for a particular field. Say you are looking at becoming a personal trainer; you may want to search to find out what types of certifications are needed to be able to work in your community, as well as your state. Understand that many positions are government-regulated and will require some type of training in order to be able to work. Whether you decide to start your own business as a personal trainer, or whether you plan on working out of a posh gym, you will need some type of educational instruction, as well as certifications.

A word of caution: Just because you find a course online does not mean it is an established learning tool. There is still some uncharted territory when it comes to regulating and monitoring the courses you can find on the Internet. Before signing up or spending any money, it may be wise to conduct a small investigation. You can do this by typing in the particular name of the university or organization with the word "scam" next to it. If anyone has had an adverse experience with the particular organization, you may find a number of articles telling about what other users have experienced. You can also do research through the Better Business Bureau (BBB) to find out if an online course is legitimate. You can search the company name to find out if there are any problems from students or other consumers. If the business or organization is listed with the BBB, you will also be able to learn if there are any complaints — and if so, how many, what they relate to, and whether they were resolved.

To begin the process:

- Identify what skills or additional courses you will need for your job.
- Decide how much time and money you are willing to commit to the class.
- Search for companies or institutions, which offer courses you need.
- Research the company or institution to ensure they are legitimate.
- Enroll in the course or class.

Finding and Pursuing New Career Alternatives

Now that you have a good handle as to how to organize yourself for you search and where to find job leads, you may want to think about pursuing your true dreams, in terms of new possible careers. Are you thinking about becoming an accountant because you have heard they make good money, or are you thinking about becoming a music instructor because you feel very passionate about that particular artistic venue? With the Internet, a mere pipe dream can become reality. Through the World Wide Web, you can research the types of credentials you will need to become a professional music instructor. You may even be able to take some accredited courses online, thus fine-tuning you skills to get you one step closer to your dream job.

You may want to begin your journey by:

- Researching the field you are interested in by visiting some of the larger Web sites that are specific to the industry

- Taking a look at some of the companies in the industry by visiting their Web sites

- Learning what their mission statement is and finding out about their goals and objectives

- Looking at some of their job listings to determine what are core requirements and skills that are necessary to get into the field

- Deciding on what courses or classes you want to take in order to bring you closer to your dream job

CHAPTER 5

*Using Internet Resources for Résumés,
Cover Letters, and Other Items*

Internet Lingo

Cover letter: A letter addressed to a potential employer, written by a job candidate. The correspondence usually includes the fact that the job seeker is applying for the position and provides details as to why the candidate is the best person for the position.

Curriculum vitae (CV): A document that lists a job seeker's basic contact information: name, address, e-mail address, phone number, work history, and experience. The document is usually more extensive than a résumé. A CV also allows individuals to expand on any academic or teaching experience they may have, as well as any honors they received, publications or articles attributed to them, or any significant achievements they have made in their life.

File: Usually a document that is made on your computer, like a résumé or a cover letter. In a computer, when you save a document, it becomes a file.

Font: A particular style of typeface setting used to create a document. Most résumés are done in a Times New Roman style, with a 12-point size, with both regular and bold words.

Grammar check: A tool that can be used to check the grammar of a particular document.

Margins: The spacing you have at the top, bottom, left, and right sides of your document. The default margins on most documents are one inch on the top and bottom, and 1.25 inches on the left and right sides of the document.

Page setup: The settings for how you arrange your document. It can include the margins, the paper size, and whether the document is going to be formatted for landscape (horizontal) or vertical viewing.

Portfolio: A collection of work or materials created, developed, or prepared by a job candidate. The portfolio can include written articles, photographs, or any other type of material that the job seeker can showcase to a potential employer.

Résumés: A document that lists a job seeker's basic information, such as name, address, e-mail address, and phone number, as well as work history, achievements, education, and past job responsibilities.

Spell check: A tool that can be used to check the spelling of a particular document.

Tools: The various formatting, developing, and editing resources available to you when creating a document or file. One of the most important tools is the capability to click on your computer and conduct a spelling and grammar check of your entire document.

The next step in applying for your jobs is to create or organize the materials — or tools — you will need. The Internet is your source for information regarding résumés, designing cover letters, and other items that you may want to have on hand for particular job types.

You may rework the documents based on the particular jobs you are applying for, but you must start with your originals. You are going to be judged, at least initially, by your tools, such as your résumé and cover letter. This is your time to shine. Careful thought should also go into what your tools are going to look like.

Using Technology to Design Your Résumé(s)

There was a time when plainly stating your work experience and credentials helped you land a job. Because of technology and the ease of applying for jobs online, though, so much has changed, including what employers are looking for in a résumé. Now you are competing with potentially thousands of other job applicants in the online arena, and it is crucial that your résumé dazzle your employer.

The Internet can help you find résumé styles you would like to use, samples of cover letters, and tips for emphasizing your key attributes and qualities to employers, as well as instructions on designing a **portfolio** of your work.

Through your résumé and cover letters, potential employers will get to know you. That is why it is so important to take the time to create or design a document that accentuates the important and relevant experience, education, and skills you may have acquired over the years.

If you make a mistake on either your résumé or your cover letter, you cannot go back to the employer and say, "I'm sorry, I didn't send you the right copy," or "I didn't check for spelling or grammar mistakes before I sent my material to you."

If you do not put in the effort, it will be apparent. From a potential employer's point of view, why would they want to hire someone who is careless, and who takes so little time in preparing documents? To the employer, that ultimately means those qualities will be reflected in your work, which will mean the difference between your getting hired or your staying unemployed.

Deciding on the type of résumé you need

One of the first areas you will want to tackle includes choosing what type of résumé you want to have available. You may decide that you want to have several versions of a résumé if you are looking at several different fields.

Before you begin to format your résumé, be sure to have a list of your work experience handy. You may recall making such a list and keeping it in a notebook or other safe place when you were initially organizing your job-hunt strategies. Make sure that your résumé follows a chronological order — if you are going to use that type and format. If so, you can start with your most recent job title, work experience, duties, and responsibilities, and continue your résumé until you get to the beginning of your experience.

There are several different types of résumés to choose from. Depending on your skills, experience, awards, or profession, one may suit your needs better than another. Or, you may like to craft several variations of your résumé, depending on what specific jobs and positions you are planning on applying for.

Basic résumé types include chronological, functional, combination, targeted, and curriculum vitae (CV) — which can be much longer than a résumé and more extensive, as they usually run longer than one page. Each of these types has its own advantages when it comes to applying for jobs. While most of the information will be the same on each document, it is the way the data is organized and highlighted that will determine résumé type is being used. *Actual examples of the four résumé types can be found in Appendix C.*

For example:

1. ***Chronological résumé:*** This type of résumé uses a chronological method to lay out basic information about someone. It may begin with the standard contact information (name, address, phone, e-mail), then include a brief objective. After that, your résumé will go on to include work history in chronological order. Your most recent job is outlined first, and includes your job title, the name of the company, city and state where the company is located, and your duties and responsibilities. All your other work history comes after that, again starting with your second-most-recent job, then your third, and so on. Education is usually on the bottom of your résumé and follows a chronological order, too, beginning with your most recent schooling and diploma or degree.

    For someone who has not had a lot of significant accomplishments but has had steady work history, the chronological résumé will work well, as it highlights real-life skills and experience.

2. ***Functional résumé:*** This résumé allows an individual to highlight both their skills and their experience, but changes the order of the material. Like the chronological résumé, the functional résumé will

also begin with your basic contact information and a history of your work experience. Your history, however, may or may not include dates of service, and it may not even follow the order in which you have held various jobs. Instead, the purpose of a functional résumé is to highlight and emphasize your skills and accomplishments, more so than your work history. Therefore, you may want to list your skills and accomplishments toward the top of your résumé, placing them in between your contact information and your work experience. A functional résumé can be effective if you have been out of the workforce for periods of time, but have certain credentials and accomplishments that will help you get the job.

3. *Combination résumé:* This allows an individual to highlight both their accomplishments and their work experience. Like the functional résumé, the combination résumé will include the basic contact information along with skills and accomplishments. However, the combination résumé may also include work history in the same manner as the chronological résumé. This type of résumé can be effective for an individual who has numerous accomplishments in a particular field with a work history that reflects those skills and accomplishments.

4. *Target résumé:* The individual's skills, accomplishments, and work history are all relevant to a particular job type or industry on this résumé. It will include the basic contact information, just as the other three types of résumés do. Information on a target résumé is arranged to highlight and focus on the items that are important to the particular job you are applying for, or that are important in the field you are pursuing. This résumé can be used by someone who may have held positions in various fields but had acquired relevant skills through those different jobs. It also works well for someone

who has the skills and experience for a particular job or industry, but has had jobs that were irrelevant to the position they are applying for. For example, someone applying for a medical position would not necessarily want to highlight his or her previous retail experience, but instead would show the skills he or she learned in medical school.

Length

It is useful to have several different versions of your résumé. You may want to have a one-page résumé, boiled down to just the essential experience. The single-page résumé is appropriate if lengthy credentials indicate that you may be overqualified for the position you are vying for. Single-page résumés are also used when you get the impression that your employer will not want to flip through three or four pages of your work experience. Consider the industry you are applying for — if urgency or deadlines are an important part of your job, your employer will likely be pressed for time and will not look past the first page anyway. On the other hand, you may also want to use a multiple-page résumé if you are trying to get into a particular company, or the government, where every accomplishment will be weighed in your favor, or where the employer wants to see all of the applicable experience you have in the particular field.

Style and design

The style of a résumé is not to be taken lightly. Your résumé should be an indication of the field you are trying to get a job in; it is your chance to show employers why you deserve a particular job. If you are trying to get a position in the arts or entertainment field, for example, something that has a little pizzazz may be appropriate. On the other hand, if you are applying for a position at a conservative company or government agency, you may want to stick with the basics, creating a less flashy résumé, but still including all of the pertinent information that will get you hired.

Also, if you are applying to companies that are different in nature — for example, one entertainment agency but one government agency — you may want to create a résumé that is eye-catching but subtle enough that it can be used for jobs across the board.

What to include

A well-done résumé may or may not include an objective, although most will include your education, work experience, skills, awards, and certifications.

If you do not have a great deal of work history, you may want to begin your résumé with a clear objective. The statement will indicate to an employer what direction and career path you are hoping to take.

If, on the other hand, you have a great deal of experience, you may not want to include such an objective. You may want to let your accomplishments indicate to an employer what career path you have already proved yourself in.

CASE STUDY: AGENCY AND CAREER COACH

Putting in Time and Effort Will
Pay Off
Cheryl Palmer, career coach
Call to Career
www.calltocareer.com
Phone (877) 743-9521
Fax (419) 793-6120
admin@calltocareer.com

*Spending time making sure that your résumé and cover letters are the best they possibly can be will go a long way in the hiring process. Time spent on such preparation is very worthwhile, said Cheryl Palmer, career coach and founder of Call to Career at **www.calltocareer.com**. The company specializes in assisting job seekers in finding employment, as well as finding their career niche.*

"The job candidate needs to demonstrate succinctly that he/she matches the job posting as closely as possible to get the reviewer's attention," Palmer said. "Since most résumés will be scanned into a database and will not be initially seen by a human being, candidates need to identify keywords from job postings to ensure that their résumés meet the search criteria of the recruiter or hiring manager."

Palmer adds that the same amount of work needs to go into the cover letter as well.

The cover letter needs to be tailored to each individual job that candidates apply for. A generic cover letter will look and feel generic, and employers may assume that you are not really interested in their job; you just "want" a job, she said.

Palmer, who holds a master's degree in counseling from the University of Maryland, attributes at least one problem job seekers may being experiencing in not finding employment to the lack of advance effort on the part of the candidate. Each résumé and cover letter should really grab the attention of the employer, she said.

"Think of résumés and cover letters as a sales pitch — if it's not convincing, the employer is not likely to call for an interview," she said.

Putting it On Paper

You should think strongly about investing in a program like Microsoft® Word to create your online résumé. A number of computers may not carry the program. You can check to see if yours does have the program installed. It may be a wise investment, given that most employers prefer receiving résumés and cover letters in a document form. While there may be other word processing programs, such as Pages or OpenOffice.org, there will be additional steps required to export your document as a Word file.

1. Begin by clicking the Start button located on the bottom left corner of your computer screen.
2. From there, click on "All Programs.
3. From there, see if you can locate Microsoft® Office or Microsoft® Word.
4. If it is there, go ahead and click on Word.
5. A new blank window will appear. This is where you will begin your résumé.

You should familiarize yourself with the basics of the toolbar, located at the top of your screen. You will use your toolbar to make text bold, italic, or underlined, as well as center- or right-align other text on your résumé.

You will notice that the there is a toolbar line that comprises picture icons (folders, scissors, printer, clipboards, and more). The pictures can be used as shortcuts for various computer tasks. Another toolbar, which functions as a navigation menu, presents headings, including File, Edit, View, Insert, and Format. When you click on the headings, there will be drop-down menus, allowing you to perform various computer tasks. The third line consists of both text and symbols, which can also be used to perform computer tasks and shortcuts.

You will want to begin your résumé by listing your basic contact information, which you can center at the top of the page. Notice the four picture icons of small lines on your toolbar, usually near the letters, **B**, *I*, and U̲.

If you click over each of the four-line pictures, you will be able to change the alignment of your text. The lines will look like this:

Left-aligned: This sets all of your text to be aligned at the left side of the page, meaning everything on the left will be in a straight line, while the right side will be staggered. This is the default alignment for most documents.

Center-aligned: The text will be moved so that each line is centered. While you may not want to use this format for the body of the document, it can be used in sections or for headlines, like your contact information at the top of the page, or the different categories of your résumé, like the word "Objective."

Right-aligned: This will send all of your text and lines to the right side of the page, which is not standard for most résumés or cover letters. You may, however, choose to use this alignment for small bits of information, like your employer's contact information on your cover letter.

Justified: Every line will begin on the left margin, with no indentation, and be carried over to the right as far as it will go. With this style, all of the lines in a paragraph will be made the same length — the spacing between words is adjusted. This is the type of alignment often used in newspapers and books.

For the purposes of your résumé, these steps will start with the second set of lines and center the basic contact information for your résumé. The usual default font, or print type, used in most résumés is Times New Roman. If you look on the toolbar, you should see the font names, next to a box containing numbers. The number is automatically set to 12, which is the size of the type you will be using to create your résumé. It is important to know the font size because you may want to make some text on your résumé a little larger, like your name, and you may want to shrink the type size of other parts, like the body, especially if you are just a line or two over creating a one-page résumé.

In addition to using different types of alignment, you may also want to format your name, or all of your contact information, in **bold** font. The three letters next to the text size also represent computer controls. If you click on the **B**, your text will be **bolded**. If you click on the *I*, your text will be *italicized*. If you click on the <u>U</u>, your text will be <u>underlined</u>.

You can use the bold, underline, and italics features to accentuate some areas of your résumés and to break up some of the text. Areas to make bold may include company names, titles, and your name, while you may want to underline each category of your résumé. Or, you may choose to italicize any descriptions you include about your work or education. Regardless of what font styles you choose, be careful not to overload your résumé.

Now that you have centered your contact information by clicking on the appropriate set of lines on your toolbar, you may also want to click on the **B** to make your name appear bold. You can click on the **B** again to unbold the text, if you change your mind. Once you have completed your basic contact information, you may want to click the first set of lines, which will align the rests of your text to the left margin of the page.

If you are beginning with an objective, start your next section with the word "Objective," followed by your goal in sending this résumé to the employer. If you want to make the word "Objective" bold and keep the rest of the text regular, simply highlight the word. Go up to the **B** on you toolbar and click it. If you want to underline or italicize any text, follow the same procedure, using either the *I* for italic or the U to underline. Use the following as an example:

Objective: To secure a position in the Internet Technology field where my talents as a Web content developer will be fully utilized.

If you are trying to create a one-page résumé and you find that you are over by a few lines, you may want to decrease the type size or margin size. You can decrease the type size by highlighting the entire text of the document and move the text size down to 11. If you need just a little more room, you may want to keep playing with your font size or font style, but you can also slightly adjust the margins. You can do this by clicking on file at the top of your toolbar and then moving down to the page setup selection. Go to the margins tab and make a left margin or right margin adjustment, or a top or bottom size adjustment. This will adjust the size of your résumé document and will help you fit more items on one page.

Once your résumé is complete, you will want to check it for spelling or grammatical errors. Click on Tools at the top of the menu. Click on Spelling and Grammar (your computer program may use a similar heading for this function). Make sure to read the document as you go along because the spelling and grammar tool does not pick up items such as improper word usage. For instance, if you talk about *where* you have previously used a skill, and you spell it as *wear*, the checker is not going to let you know that you used the word associated with apparel and that you should have used "where" instead. Such details show what you must be aware of in the final stages of creating your résumé. When you run a spelling and grammar check, a box will appear and bring you to the location in the document where there may be an issue, such as a misspelled word. Once there, you can choose to make a suggested change, or ignore it and move on. Just keep in mind that the checker is not always correct.

After the review has been done, you are ready to save your document and store it in your a new desktop folder. If you prefer not to create a file folder, you may also store your résumé right on your desktop for easy access.

Storing Your Files in a Safe Place

Creating a new folder on your desktop for all of your job-search tools is a good way to begin the process. Once you have your folder, you can title it something pertaining to your job search; that way, you will always have your job tools in a location that is easily accessible. You can also keep your tools in your "My Documents" folder, which is already on your computer. However, the folder may get pretty crowded with other documents, and you certainly do not want to accidentally send something else you may be storing. For example, you might accidentally send your New Year's resolution list to a potential employer because it was located in your documents folder, near your New Year Résumé document.

Steps to create a new folder
1.   Click your mouse anywhere there is free space on your desktop.
2.   Right click on your mouse. You will notice various headings and tasks.
3.   Move your cursor to the one that says "New."
4.   Click on "Folder" or "New Folder" — which will also show a picture of a folder.
5.   A new file folder will appear on your desktop.

6.	Under the picture of the folder are the words "New Folder." You want to type in the heading you will use for your folder, such as Jobs 2010, or Résumés and Cover Letters.
7.	If you missed the chance to type in the new name, or if you want to rename the folder, simply click once onto the folder title that reads "New Folder."
8.	Right click your mouse.
9.	Click on "Rename," usually located at the bottom of the listings.
10.	Rename the file and click outside the box.
11.	You are done, and you now have a brand-new desktop file folder to keep and organize all your job search and application tools.

	Saving your résumé and other documents
1.	Begin by clicking File at the top of the toolbar.
2.	You can click Save or Save As.
3.	A box will appear. At the top of the box it will say, Save As and there will be a picture of a file folder with the name of that folder, such as My Documents, or Job Search 2009.
4.	If the file folder that appears is the one that you want to save your résumé to, go to the bottom of the box where it says File Name and name the document.
5.	Click Save. Your document will be stored in the file folder.
6.	If, by chance, the top file folder is not where you want to place the document, you can change the folder location by clicking on the downward arrow next to the folder. A list of folders and items, such as Desktop, will appear. You can choose from the list before you go ahead and save your résumé.
7.	To access your résumé, all you have to do is open the file folder, such as My Documents or Job Search 2009, and double click on the file title, such as J. Smith Résumé.
8.	Your document should open.

Designing your cover letter

There are all kinds of places on the Internet where you can find tips for designing your cover letter. As you decide on a style for your cover letter, you should also decide how personal you want it to be.

There should be some basic information included in every cover letter. The essential information will include the employer's name, address, your reason for contacting the employer (in other words, your mission), and your contact information (name, address, phone number, and e-mail address).

The cover letter should appear professional and include specific information, such as the actual job title you are applying for, where you saw the advertisement for that job, and the reasons why you are the most qualified candidate to fill the position.

The standard length for such a letter should be no more than a page. Typically, employers are busy people and do not have time to flip through pages upon pages of a letter telling them why you want a job at their companies. Keep your cover letter short and sweet, but be sure to include all of the basics.

Date

When creating a professional business letter, it is accepted practice to begin with the date of the letter. If you are not indenting any paragraphs, you can place the date on the top-left corner of the document. You will want to skip a few lines before moving on to your contact person, most likely your employer or someone at the HR department of the firm you are applying to, and company address. Be sure to spell out the month, and use numerals for the date and the year. Avoid using only numerals. It should look like this: January 9, 2010.

If you are planning on using indented paragraphs, then you may want to insert your date on the top right line of the document. Just make sure to tab over enough so that the document looks attractive and balanced. You can also set your document alignment for the "date" line to be right-aligned; that way, you do not have to worry about tabbing over too far or too little.

Company, contact name, and company address

It is always better to personalize your cover letter. *Dear Ms. Smith* or *Dear Mr. Jones* always sounds better than *Dear Madam* or *Dear Sir*, or than *To Whom it May Concern.* These are impersonal and do not give a genuine, sincere appearance. Usually, the only time it is acceptable to be so vague is if a job advertisement specifically indicates to respond that way. Otherwise, use a name. If you are unable to find a name, use *Dear Human Resources Representative*, if you must.

Sometimes finding the name of the person who is handling the job posting can be like finding a needle in a haystack. Some companies go to great lengths on the Internet to protect themselves from unsolicited inquiries from sales representatives as well as job seekers. Sometimes a company Web site simply does not have the information because it is a basic site, with few bells and whistles.

If the information is not easily accessible, meaning there is no one's name attached to the job posting, you may want to go to the company Web site and conduct your own research. Sometimes the information can be found under company or corporate officers tabs, in which you can use the name affiliated with the human resources or human capital division. Many times, however, if you go to a particular company Web site, you can also find the name by clicking on the company overview or the "about us" link on the site.

Company addresses can be found the same way, usually by clicking on the contact link. If you are still unable to find the address, go to the online White Pages (**www.whitepages.com**) and type in the company name, city, and state.

You must be a resourceful job seeker. You must show your potential employer that you are capable of handling the little tasks, like finding information about a company online, as well as the larger ones, such as finding out which companies may have secured additional government funding, or which firms have procured large scale contracts. After you have located both the address and the name of the person you are sending your letter to, you must come up with the text or body of the cover letter.

Job title and advertisement

You want to begin your letter by letting the employer know what position you are applying for, where you found the job advertisement, and what date you saw the ad. While applying to a particular job may be the only item on your agenda, human resources employees in particularly large companies are faced with hundreds of job postings on any given day. This means that your résumé and cover letter are just one of those submissions, so you not only need to set yourself apart, but you need to be straightforward. Be clear as to which position you are applying for and what the job title is, as well as where you saw the job advertisement, so human resources employees can match you with the job opening you are actually applying for. Try wording the beginning of your cover letter like the following:

Dear Ms. Williams:

I am asking to be considered for the position of Senior Customer Service Representative, as prefaced in your advertisement on HotJobs, dated January 1, 2009.

Qualifications, skills, accomplishments, and personal objectives

Once you have stated clearly which position you are applying for, you want to move on to explain why you are a good fit for the position. You will want to include your qualifications, credentials, and skills that are relevant to the position you are applying for. In addition, if you have made accomplishments in the field, you will want to include them. Remember: The more specific the accomplishments, the better the decision-maker will be able to determine whether you are a good fit for the job.

This is also where you want to include any relevant keywords or phrases from the job advertisement and the industry. You may also want to include language from the company's Web site or mission statement. You need to show a potential employer you are savvy not only in terms of the industry, but in terms of the skills and experience in which the employer is seeking to hire someone.

The same keywords you included in your résumé can be used in your cover letter, too. But, while the résumé provides a listing or a summary of your credentials, it is through the cover letter that you can personalize yourself more to a potential employer. While they employer may first check to see if you have the skills and experience for the job through your résumé, they will look to the cover letter to find your personalized pitch as to why you are the most knowledgeable and best candidate for the position. Thus, even though your résumé and cover letter are similar in nature, your cover letter gives you the opportunity to expand on your knowledge of industry buzzwords, important skills, and related work experience.

If you are applying for a particular position, such as a grant writer, you may want to be as specific as possible when mentioning your accomplishments. This advice holds particularly true when it comes to financial matters. Most employers are concerned with the bottom line. If you have been successful in bringing in funds, saving the company money, or any other way that contributes to the company's goal, potential employers want to know about it. Look at the following vague example:

As a grant writer, I was successful in working on numerous state and federal grants.

You want to make sure you go into as much detail as you can. This is not the time to be modest or subtle, particularly when talking about helping a company achieve its goals. This example is better:

I was successful in securing $250,000 for my company through the state grant program (name the program). I was also instrumental in securing an additional $500,000, through the federal grant program (name the program).

Of course, you could also list the specific grant programs, as well as what the funds were subsequently used for. Regardless of how you decide to do it, you need to show your employers that you are the best person for the job. You may want to clarify your own intentions: You are looking to find a position with a company where there is room for growth and advancement. Or, maybe you are looking to align yourself with a company where your skills and talents will be fully utilized for team accomplishments.

Closer

Use good etiquette to thank the individual who is taking the time to read your application and your letter. You will also want to indicate that you are anxious to speak to him or her about the posting and your candidacy for the job. Expressing your interest and gratitude is important for any cover letter, regardless of the type of job you are applying for. Use the following as an example:

Thank you in advance for your time and attention in the matter of my application. I would greatly appreciate the opportunity to speak with you about my candidacy, and the expertise I can bring to the table in terms of credentials. I look forward to hearing from you.

You will want to sign your letter in a professional matter as well. Using words such as *sincerely* or *respectfully yours* are both good ways to end a cover letter.

In putting the finishing touches on your cover letter, it should be pointed out that you should also have your contact information on your cover letter. You may want to include it at the top of the page, if you designed your résumé that way. The information should include your name, address, e-mail address, and phone numbers. Be sure to use some sort of visual or design technique, such as spacing or inserting a line, to separate your contact information from the rest of the cover letter, if you are including it near the top of your letter. Or, you can simply include it under your name, at the bottom of the letter.

Creating a Personalized Digital Portfolio

For some positions, you may want to consider creating a personalized digital portfolio from which you can send items to potential employers.

You can store any items that may be relevant to securing your next position in the folder you created on your computer for your job search. These items might include scanned or online copies of accomplishments, awards, certifications, and other materials you have created or developed during your educational or work years.

Sometimes potential employers will want to see examples of the skills and experience you demonstrate in your résumé and cover letter. That is when you can reach into your digital portfolio and attach documents and images that will speak volumes of your worth and the quality of your work.

Why you need one

Many employers are looking beyond the résumé to determine whether a person is going to be an asset or a liability for a particular company. If the employer hires the wrong individual, there are consequences, from having to let the person go, to having a vacancy that burdens other workers, and to going through the process all over again for finding a new employee.

Employers like to see results, and they like to see proof. Therefore, most employers want to see more than a résumé to show them what a job candidate is capable of accomplishing. Through the use of the digitalized portfolio, the employer will have this proof. For example, an individual who is looking to work as a project supervisor for a craft store would want to show that he or she is capable of being able to make crafts and give design instructions for others who are making crafts.

If you were a savvy Internet job seeker who has the right credentials for the craft job, and you have a digitalized portfolio, you could simply select a few photos of the crafts you have completed, along with the copies of the instructions you had designed. These could be sent to your potential employer to set yourself aside from other candidates, and to increase your chances of getting the job.

If you are a writer or photographer, the digitalized portfolio is a standard tool that has proved its worth. For example, if you are a writer, you will want to store copies of your writings or articles in a digitalized portfolio, where you can send your samples to potential employers with minimal effort. As a photographer, your photos are your credentials and can be organized with an online portfolio. You will also want to have easy access to be able to send copies through the Internet, not copies through the mail. If you are not pursuing a career in either field, the portfolio could be just as valuable a tool for you. If, for instance, you are opting for a chef's position at a fine restaurant, what better way to showcase your entrées than with a photo of the finished delight? Or, if you are an educator, perhaps scanning some of your favorite school projects and curriculum would help to motivate an employer your way.

Types of portfolios

There are various types of digitalized portfolios, and you will have to decide which one works best for your needs. There are types of portfolios for learning, which are used by students and educators, while others highlight your work. Other portfolios are designed to warehouse your credentials or your plans for the future. For the purposes of a job seeker, you may want to focus on a combination of the different types that will include your accomplishments, projects, and progress.

The types of documents to be included would be any awards you may have received for past performance in jobs or school, documents that you prepared regarding a specific project, photographs of your finished products, documentation regarding your progression for particular skills, and any letters of praise or accolades you have received from customers, clients, or prior supervisors. You may also want to include information about the progress of your job search activities. This is important, for example, if you have attended a career fair and made contact with a representative from a company you are interested in applying to. You will want to refer to the particular event, along with its outcome, if you decide to apply for a job with that particular company. You will want to mention the person whom you met, and when and where the event was held.

It is important to remember that your digital portfolio can simply be compiled as a text document, or you can use a design program to gather everything on your computer. If you choose to create your portfolio on your own computer, you can e-mail the files or document to your employer.

You can use a social networking Web site or blog to create your portfolio, too. With this method, you would upload your files to the site and simply include the link to the page in your résumé or cover letter. *For more information about using social networking sites, see Chapter 8.*

How to do it

Because your digitalized portfolio will be stored on you computer, you will need to begin by gathering the materials you want to include. Some of these may already exist as files on your computer, and others may be items like articles, proposals, or pictures that you have to scan into your computer. If you happen to have a printer with scanning capabilities, you can scan the documents and pictures.

Regardless of where the files are coming from, you should save them all in a similar place. Follow the steps described earlier for creating a new folder on your desktop — it is a good idea to have a separate folder for your portfolio items so you do not have to search every folder on your computer for the things you want to send to your potential employer each time you apply for a job.

From there, you will be able to access the document or photograph and send it to any potential employer based on the job you are applying for. Like the photos are to a photographer, your work is, in this case, your credentials. The employer will have a first-hand look at how well you are able to perform.

What to include

Think of your work and what you are most proud of. Think of the awards or certificates you have received in the past. Perhaps your biggest accomplishments occurred some time ago. Or, maybe you cannot go into enough detail about them on your résumé. Those items can be included in your digital portfolio. If you completed a particular class that is essential to a particular job, include the certificate in your digital portfolio. If you have never won an award, or received any course credit or certification, you may want to leave this out. However, you may also want to think outside the box. Is there a hobby that is relevant? Have you done any community service that is relevant? You may want to design a special form or document that is targeted to your accomplishments in the particular field or profession you are interested in.

The material should represent you in the best and most favorable light. This is your time to thoroughly shine. If you cannot explain it in words, try a photograph. But remember to filter your personal achievements from your professional ones. While you may be proud of the fact you caught the largest trout all season, the picture of you holding your catch does not belong in the portfolio — unless, of course, you are looking to get into the bait and tackle business. Again, keep everything professional.

Additional things you may want to include are:

- Job performance reviews and assessments
- Attendance at professional conferences or workshops
- Speaking engagements where you were the speaker
- Mentions in local news stories or company newsletters
- Letters of recommendation from past employers or clients
- Scores from skills assessments tests (if they were good)

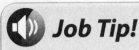

Job Tip!

If you happen to be unemployed and are conducting a job search, you may be eligible for unemployment benefits. Most states require you to conduct an active job search and to document your information. Having that data easily accessible and organized will be a time-saver.

Techniques to Simplify the Application Process

You should know some of the basics about cutting and pasting résumés and cover letters. Unless you want to rewrite your résumé numerous times, the quickest way is to have it handy in the folder you created on your desktop — this way, you can copy and paste it when the job site prompts you to insert a résumé.

The pictures at the top of the toolbar all serve a purpose. You can use them to carry out many of the steps in preparing and saving a document. Take, for instance, the blank white box at the top left corner of the tool bar. If you click on it, you will open a new document. If you want to save your document, you can click on the icon picture of the small brown disk. If you want to print your document, simply click on the picture of the printer.

There are other handy shortcuts, as well. Take the scissors, for example. If you decide you want to cut a line or a paragraph out of a document, simply highlight the area and click on the scissors. Your text will be stored in the "cut" memory. If you want to copy but not remove a particular portion of a document, highlight the text and click on the duplication papers located to the right of the scissors on the top of your tool bar, if you are using Microsoft Word, for instance. The same capability may not be available on other computers or programs. If you need to paste the text in another location on the document, just click the area of the screen where you want to insert the text and click on the clipboard at the top of your tool bar. You have cut, copied, and pasted in about 10 seconds flat, versus having to type the entire document from scratch.

What parts can be copied for all jobs

Some of the parts that you will be able to copy and paste may include your contact information, your education, and experience. From there, you can always tailor your objective and skill sets to highlight particular talents to each employer.

Say you have a very solid work background in a particular field. You notice that the skills requirements for a particular position are tasks you have performed but are not completely highlighted or reflected through your work experience. It is more of a problem because you have a very nice chronological style résumé that does not even mention any of the skills required for the new job.

This is where knowing how to cut and paste comes in handy. You may want to put together a new résumé — but this time, you will use a combination style. Copy and paste your basic contact information at the top of the page, then you can create a list of skills right under the contact information. You can create the list, using your own skills and matching them up with the required skills.

Once that step is done, you can refer to your original résumé and copy your work experience, which you will paste right after your skills section. With a few adjustments, you now have a combination résumé, and you have successfully accentuated the skills that are important to the potential employer. If your résumé is too long, you may want to cut some of the job responsibilities or duties you performed in your previous jobs. You start with cutting the things that are the least relevant to the job.

What parts should be specific to each job

Sometimes your résumé should be more specific to the particular job you are applying for. Take, for instance, a job as an information technology (IT) professional. If the advertisement calls for a specific set of skills, then you should make sure to highlight those skills and duties from any prior job in which you performed them.

Keep in mind that a job title may mean one thing to one employer or company, but still have a different meaning to another company. In these cases, you want to make sure that your résumé includes duties and responsibilities that are specific to the particular job you are applying for. For example, if your résumé states you are a public relations and marketing professional, and you are applying for a job in the entertainment field, you may want to make your résumé as specific as possible to ensure that the employer knows you are indeed qualified for the position. Remember: You want to translate your marketing and public relations skills and experience into terms that will stick out to an entertainment executive or employer.

The following is a sample excerpt of a résumé created by someone with marketing experience who is applying for a position in the arts and entertainment industry:

Hosted numerous high-profile events, which were attended by national and regional musicians. Worked on the pre-publicity for the 2008 Music Awards, which was attended by 2,000 guests and carried a TV viewing audience of 2 million.

Sending Your Job Tools

Because most employers and job postings call for submitting a résumé, you must develop a document that can be saved and stored in your computer.

You may want to scan the document into your computer, or create a résumé on your computer using programs such as Microsoft® Word. Either way, you must first learn how to send a résumé, as well as a cover letter, to a potential employer.

Sending a hard copy, or paper résumé, through the mail can take several days. Sometimes, company addresses and whom to "attention" the document to are not readily available through the general online job posting. You may have to check several different sources to find the address, particularly if you are applying to a company or corporation with multiple office locations. While you are busy mailing off the necessary paperwork, scores of other job applicants are beating you to the punch.

But, it certainly would not hurt to go one step further than your competitors by sending your material through the Internet in addition to mailing a copy of your résumé, your cover letter, and a personal note. That way, your future employer will see, first-hand, that you do know your way around the Internet and are conscientious about making sure all your bases are covered.

CHAPTER 6

Research Before You Apply

Internet Lingo

About Us: For purposes of job hunting, the "About Us" section of a Web site is the introduction or a summarized version of the company, what it does, and what its history is. You can usually find it by clicking on a labeled hyperlink on the top, side, or bottom of a Web page.

Better Business Bureau (BBB): A private, nonprofit organization whose mission is to promote and foster the highest ethical relationship between consumers and businesses. The organization also keeps records on companies in good standing, as well as those with complaints lodged against them.

Company philosophy: Usually the reasons why the company was formed, why it is in business, or how it conducts business.

Hoover's, Inc. (www.hoovers.com): An established company that specializes in corporate research. Information from a company's size to the number of employees and corporate officers can be found through the site.

Mission: The reason that a company exists. This is a company's purpose in the business world, and the main drive behind its goals and objectives.

OneSource (www.onesource.com): A company that warehouses similar business information as that found with Hoover's, Inc. The organization's products include such items as a business browser full of corporate data.

Before you make any kind of significant purchase, you usually conduct some level of research to find out what you are getting in return for your investment. Sometimes you will shop around to get the best deal, rather than buying the first item you find; that way, you avoid what is known as buyer's remorse — an unfulfilled feeling after purchasing a product you did not really want. To remedy the situation, you are going to have to go out and invest in something new if your needs are to be met.

Applying blindly to a company or a government agency without first conducting research can leave you in the same predicament, but with more severe consequences. For example, if you are interested in fashion retail and ultimately want to become a buyer at a department store, you should research related companies before you start applying for jobs. You may apply to a position titled "buyer," and later learn that the job and company have nothing at all to do with fashion. You may find yourself doing the buying for eco-friendly cleaning products, sending yourself away from your dream job and goals.

Or, say that you do find a position that is the right fit, but with a company you have not even passively researched. For the sake of argument, say the position is for a supervisor of a medium-sized company. The pay was in your range, and the commute was perfect, but what you did not know — because you did not conduct any research — is that the company is soon going under. Your position is temporary, at best. Because of numerous layoffs the company has conducted in the last year, you are expected not only to do the work of several supervisors, but you are responsible for ensuring that the demoralized, unhappy workers under your supervision pull double-duty as well. It is not an enviable position for anyone to be in, let alone someone who is looking for long-term job security.

There are also long-term consequences to such issues. If you decide to leave the position, you will have to start your job search all over again. If you opt to leave without helping the company fill your position, you may be left without a good reference, in addition to your dire financial situation as you go back to being unemployed.

Be "In The Know" Before You Apply

Conducting active, or even passive, company research can go a long way in helping you to secure a position that is the right fit for you. When you stop to consider that most jobs involve a 40-hour workweek, you want to spend that time feeling satisfied and comfortable. After all, the time translates into 12,000 minutes a week, or 4,380,000 minutes a year. The time can feel like eternity if you are ill-equipped to handle the situation, or if you are just unhappy. For example, if your dream job consists of a small company environment where individualism and creativity are recognized and rewarded, you will want to work in a place where the office rules are somewhat relaxed, the dress code is casual, and time schedules are nowhere near as important as the work itself.

So, in hopes of finding your dream job, you blindly submit a résumé without researching the company, and somehow land the job. Once there, you find that you are expected to dress in "business professional" attire every day; your supervisor has you signing in and out every time you leave your cubicle; you are expected to meet daily quotas; and you are given a canned script and an encyclopedia-sized book of directives that you must follow to the tee while performing even the most menial task. How well would you do in such an environment? Job satisfaction, needless to say, would be low. Few could flourish under those types of circumstances.

But, if you had done your homework, you would have found that another particular company had just received a large contract and was looking to expand. Through your research, you learned that the company is very supportive of its employees, and you gain a feeling of pride from both management and the workers. You may find that the work environment is one that you could envision yourself flourishing in for years to come. Once you rework your cover letter — to include a brief mention of their recent contract award, as well as other little facts you have picked up in your research — a company may find that you are the perfect fit for them. It is a mutually rewarding relationship because the employer is impressed that you have taken the time to learn about the operation and to keep abreast of what is important to them. If there are multiple candidates for the position, your résumé and cover letter may be placed at the top of the pile because of your insider knowledge and the fact you are already up-to-speed about the company and its needs.

Using a company's home page

Find out what you are getting into before you apply. The time spent doing this will go a very long way in ensuring you are in the most optimum position for success, rather than in a setup for failure. Through such thoughtful

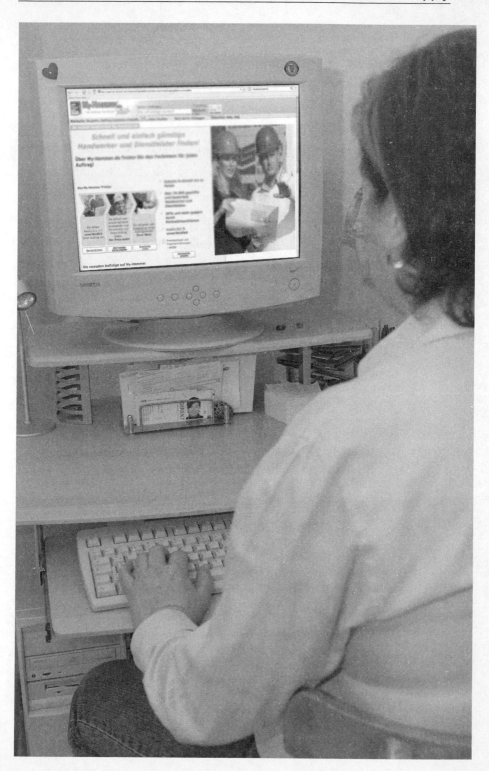

steps, you will be able to take your career to the next level, particularly if the working conditions are right, the **company philosophy** and **mission** is something important to you, and the company or agency shows stability for the future.

Begin with the most basic steps for an Internet search. For example, if you apply to a position through a search engine or a job site, the name of the company is usually listed somewhere on the job advertisement. In many instances, the job application may be connected to a link from Monster. com or Indeed.com. Once you click on the link, you will be rerouted to the company's own Web site to complete the application process.

While you are there, look for areas where you will find valuable information regarding the company. Start with the **About Us** section. This section usually provides a brief description of the company's history, the names of executives, titles, and sometimes profiles. There should also be information on the type of company it is. Under other links, you will find the products and services that the company offers. Try to determine if there are any ongoing projects that you could contribute to. What are their goals and objectives for the coming years? Do you have any specific skills or experience that would help the company achieve their goals? If so, you may want to take two approaches to the issue. First, you may want to again incorporate some keywords or phrases regarding specific tasks or skills in your résumé and your cover letter. Two, you may want to prepare a one-page statement acknowledging the ongoing project and addressing the skills you could bring to the table, if hired. You could also make a reference to the ongoing project, letting a potential employer know you have prepared a brief outline in connection with the project. It may be the extra step that catapults you ahead of the rest of the job seekers.

Be sure to read the press releases found on a company Web site. Do their employees receive any kind of recognition for achievements? Are the press releases simply quotes from the chief executive officer (CEO)? Do the employees participate in any type of charity work? Are their efforts recognized? These are just some of the areas you will want to visit to get an idea of what it is like at a particular company you are applying to.

Company profiles on other sites

If you are applying for a position through CareerBuilder.com or Monster.com, to name a few, these sites sometimes carry Web links profiling the company, as well as what to expect as an employee. The profiles are sometimes flimsy, but other times they are chock-full of valuable information that includes insight about corporate and employee workdays, benefits, and other company perks.

You can also post a question on a public forum. Take, for instance, City-data at **www.city-data.com**. The site provides profiles of communities throughout the United States. You can go to the site and post the question of whether anyone knows what it is like to work at a particular company. You can also post similar inquiries through Twitter and Yahoo!

Back to the basics

You may want to conduct a basic search for the company to learn about its reputation from a third-party perspective. If you are looking for an unbiased opinion, or just for more information than is included on the company's Web site, another easy way to research a company is to go to a search engine, such as Yahoo! or Google, and type in the company name and search.

By doing this, you should see a variety of links relating to the particular company. You can focus on business-related items, such as articles mentioning whether the company had enjoyed a profit or suffered a loss recently. You can use Google for a new search, or to be sent news alerts when stories of interest are posted. Or, you can find out what experts and others are saying about the company. This is particularly useful for a local company or firm. Sites such as Yelp (**www.yelp.com**) and Citysearch (**http:// national.citysearch.com**) carry reviews of the businesses. The reviews are usually created by customers and clients who have had contact with the particular business. The sites provide users and visitors the opportunity to write a review, good or bad. You can also click on the company Web site to find newsworthy articles, which might be listed under newsworthy articles or the media section.

One of the oldest business research sites, **Hoover's, Inc. (www.hoovers. com**), is another option for learning about a company you are applying to. Users can find basic information about a company free of charge. The type of information may include a basic description of the company, whether the company is publicly or privately owned, what the previous year's earnings were, the official address of the business, and approximately how many employees work at the company. Information including press releases, the names of top-level executives, and a profile of the company's competition can also be found. For a fee, additional details of the company are also available, as well as books profiling companies. The range goes from free to several hundred dollars.

Another resource for job seekers is the **Better Business Bureau (www.bbb. org**). This site may be particularly helpful for a local company or a company with several listed locations. Sometimes the Better Business Bureau (BBB) will break down information as it relates to each location. The BBB is an organization dedicated to advancing an ethical marketplace for all who participate. If you are concerned about a particular company, you may visit the BBB to find out the following information: whether the government has taken any action against the company, the number of consumer complaints, whether the company has a BBB accreditation, and whether the organization is in current good standing.

OneSource (**www.onesource.com**) is another informational site. Viewers can sign up for free trial access if they are looking for information on company executives, business and corporate profiles, and industry research as well. You can find out what the company does, as well as what it provides in terms of services and products. There is also a fee attached for more extensive access to the information.

You can also stop at Craigslist and post a similar question on one of the site's forums. The visiting public is usually more localized than the larger sites. You may even find suggestions as to what to do once you are hired by a specific company.

What You Should Try to Learn

Companies usually let you know upfront what is important to them, but there are times when the information is buried away in a report on their Web site as well — or in places that are not even linked to the company's Web site. To get a comprehensive picture of the company, you need to know what to look for when you research.

Determine what is important to the company

You have already found the company's vision or mission statement, probably on its home page, or on the "About Us" or "Mission" links. Everything the company does is designed around that vision or mission statement. The information may be on the first web page or under the headings regarding the company itself. Under that, you may find the company's goals and objectives. These are the steps the company is taking in order to achieve that mission or vision.

Because the most important business of a company, no matter what the product or service, is contained in the vision or mission statement, you may want to consider taking keywords or phrases from those areas and incorporating them into your own résumé and cover letter. Doing this will show your potential employer that you are in-tune with the goals of the company. It also demonstrates your ability to research and suggests you are interested in the position because of the company, not just because you need a job.

Current events

Also be sure to take the time to find out if an agency has made recent headlines. Unfortunately, more times than not, when a government agency makes front-page news, it is not because the organization is doing an outstanding job. In fact, while many agencies are outstanding, you may only see them in the news when something goes wrong.

When a particular agency is facing some kind of crisis, it can be a very public problem — unlike a private company, where the news is sometimes kept under wraps. With taxpayers footing the bill of salaries and services of these government agencies, more focus is placed on the trials and tribulations of the public sector.

Again, read everything you can on an agency Web site. If you are looking at a state government position, you may also want to read information contained on both the legislative Web site, as well as the governor's Web site. While there may be a difference of opinion in some areas, most of the highest ranking, executive-level members are appointed by the governor. If it is important to the governor, chances are it is important to the agency. On the federal level, the same can be said, to some extent.

Company stability

Some companies are very transparent, meaning that just about everything you ever wanted to know about them is out there for public consumption. Other companies are not so forthcoming about their profits and stability, for various reasons.

Again, you may want to start with your search engine and type in the company's name, as well as the word "profit." Chances are there will be numerous links to stories and articles related to the company's profits. Read everything you can. Read the news clips. Read the press releases. Read what others are saying about the company. In your research, did you find that the organization has gone through a recent series of layoffs? What was the reason for the layoffs? Does it appear that there will be more layoffs in the future?

For example, if an automobile manufacturer opts to discontinue a particular car model, there may be a number of people who can transition from one division to another, even though the jobs for building that specific car model will be lost. Are there still employees who are still working on the discontinued line, fulfilling past orders? If so, what will happen when they complete the task? Will they be absorbed into the rest of the company, or will they find themselves without a job? In many situations, the earliest ones in the door — the newest employees — are the first to face the layoffs.

In your research, you may have to act as a detective, gathering and studying information about a corporation. Do not forget to search sites such as Forbes.com or MSN.com. Type in the company name and search. The company's report or standings on Wall Street may have received recent coverage because of a good or poor performance, or because of a profitable or losing quarter. Again, stay on top of the issues, particularly those that relate to your job search and future.

Special Situations: Government Agencies and Public Sectors

There is not a lot of guesswork when it comes to government agencies. They clearly state their intentions publicly, especially when it comes to visions, missions, goals, and objectives. However, they may not be quite as savvy when it comes to posting such information on the Internet. While companies have been using Web sites for a number of years, the government, or public sector, is relatively new when it comes to Internet use for job placement. It was not so long ago when paper applications were the only forms submitted for a local, state, or even national job application. Every day, more and more effort is being placed on the public sector Web sites.

If, for example, you find a federal job on USAJobs.gov that you would like to apply to, one of the first steps you may want to take is to visit the agency's Web site. You can use your search engine to type in the name of the U.S. agency, department, commission, or organization, and conduct your search.

Once there, look to see if there is some message from the top-level executive. You can usually find this heading under corporate officers. Because public entities come under much more scrutiny than a private company, key points of the agency, its purpose, and its directives can usually be found in the welcoming statement to site visitors.

Online newspapers may also carry recent events about a particular government agency or organization. You can go to the newspaper Web site and conduct a search by typing in the name of the agency. Any relevant stories containing information about the agency should pop up. If not, you may want to click on the archives of the Web site. You may find stories that are relevant but older than three or six months. It varies from newspaper to newspaper.

From here, you may want to focus on articles mentioning whether the particular agency is planning on hiring additional workers. You may also find out whether or not the organization or department is under a hiring freeze. Researching these things will save time and energy when deciding on which public sector jobs you will be applying for.

Is there a government budget?

As it was pointed out before, sometimes there is more information to be found on a pubic sector site than a private site, and there are times when the information is pretty slim. It may also vary from agency to agency, or from one branch of the government to another. It depends on factors such as how much public funds have been dedicated to developing a particular Web site, as well as how much importance an agency decides to place on their own Web site.

In some cases, information regarding a government budget — specifically in connection to particular agencies — is very dominant and easily accessible. You may find it through an annual budget link on the Web site. Because the information is so public, and because most budgets must first pass a series of legislative and executive government approval, there is little an entity can hide.

Items in the budget may include how much the agency has to spend on new employees or new hires. That does not mean, however, that the information will be easy to find. It may be buried under a document hundreds of pages thick. The trick will be to locate the particular agency and find the annual appropriation or operating budget. Again, you may have to visit a congressional or state legislative site to find the answer.

 Job Tip!

Using the Find tool on your computer may save you some reading. For example, if you are trying to find the "Annual Budget" section in a document that is 400 pages long, go to the top of your screen and click on the word "Edit." From there, click on "Find," located next to a pair of binoculars. Type in the words "Annual Budget" and click "Find Next." The tool will bring you to the exact spot where the words are located in the document.

Using the Information You Find

Once you locate the information, feel free to incorporate it into your cover letter, or a one-page summary. You may also be able to pick up key phrases from the statement and include it in your résumé. You may want to include the information to indicate that you are well-versed in what the organization does and what is important to them. Because an agency is so public, there should be various locations where you can find additional information. You can look at some of the sites dedicated to providing information about a particular city or town. Sometimes Chambers of Commerce Web sites will contain such information. Take, for instance, the Florida Chamber of Commerce (**www.flchamber.com**), which provides insight into the business climate as well as a section on the quality of life.

If you have your heart set on finding a government job in New Orleans, for example, you may want to start out at the city's government Web site, **www.cityofno.com**. In addition to finding job opportunities, you will also be able to view projects and plans that the city is currently focused on, and what the city, as a whole, deems important. From there, you may also want to incorporate some of that knowledge and some keywords and phrases into your job search and application tools. You can begin with the welcome link from the mayor's office before turning to other parts of the page. If you use the search capacity at the top of the page and type the words "mission statement," a bevy of links connected to mission statements from various departments will pop up. You can click on the appropriate links.

Stay up-to-date on local happenings, as well as state and federal issues. They all may be connected in one form or another. The American Recovery and Reinvestment Act of 2009, for example, are connected to all states; even though the law itself was defined in Washington, the repercussions of the legislation reached across the country. The Act included the distribution of millions upon millions of dollars for the creation of jobs. You may not have had a chance to read the document, which is hundreds of pages long, but it may mean new funds for state and local agencies — which, in turn, can translate into new jobs.

Regardless of where you are submitting your résumé and cover letter, it is important that you know what type of company you are applying to, that you understand what their products and services are all about, and that the job situation is one you will feel confident in. If you are requested for an interview, you will be received more favorably if you are able to speak about the company and what it does. The more knowledge you have, the better the interview will go. To a potential boss, you will come across as the person who is savvy, well-informed, and prepared.

CHAPTER 7

How Companies and Staffing Agencies
Choose Candidates

Internet Lingo

Application: An online document or process where a job candidate may fill out a regular job form, but may also include a résumé and cover letter.

Intranet: A company network, whereby usually only the employees and those affiliated with a particular company can access the information on it. You usually have to be approved for access to sign in. While you may be able to access the network from any computer, it may be internal and not accessible to other Internet users.

PDF (Portable Document File): A file that can be created using Adobe Acrobat, and that can be printed and read, but usually not altered, copied, or edited without permission from the owner.

Security clearance: A type of status that allows the individual to access certain levels of confidential material or locations. The clearance process is usually initiated by the government, or a company doing business with the military or the government. The process involves an investigation into someone's past.

Turnover: In the hiring or employment world, it pertains to investing in and hiring an employee who subsequently leaves their position, causing the process of finding and hiring another employee to replace the one who left begins all over again.

Companies and staffing agencies use different means to locate qualified candidates using the Internet. For some companies, applicants can find the job posting and apply right on the particular organization's Web site. Usually you can find other information about the company, depending on how large the Web site is and how much detail and space it devotes to human resources or human capital issues.

For the most part, job applicants are competing with other outside candidates when it comes to Internet applications. Many companies have what is known as an **Intranet** for present employees. The Intranet not only carries a lot of the same news and information as the Internet, but the network can only be seen by company employees and those permitted access by signing into the site. Companies use the Intranet to allow present employees to apply internally for positions within the organization, such as a promotion. The site is usually also used to provide internal and external news to employees and others affiliated with the company.

While you may find a job through a major search engine, what you are really finding is the hyperlink that takes you back to the original job posting. For example, say you are looking to apply for a position at the University of Texas, San Antonio (UTSA). You may start by clicking on the hyperlink, which will lead you back to the UTSA site. From there, you may want to search for jobs or employment. You may receive several types of articles or pages dealing with employment issues. Then, when the page dealing with job openings and human resources opens, you can go ahead and click it.

For many sites, you will have to register before submitting your application. You can usually take a look at the other available positions the university or company has open by filling in information regarding location, department, or job title. If there is a way or means to set up a job agent, which will e-mail you about potential jobs in your field as they are posted, set one up.

Some companies will also limit the number of applications you can submit during a specific time period. Just because you may want to work in a particular company does not mean that you should fill out five different applications during a five-week period. By limiting the number of times candidates can submit their résumés and applications, companies will limit the number of unqualified candidate applications they have to review in order to get to the individuals who are actually suited for the job.

Often, companies will want to know who is applying at their establishment to make sure that the person who is applying is not a solicitor. While some companies like to keep the hiring process internal — within their own human resources department — other companies like to have a staffing agency serve as the first wave in weeding out the unqualified candidates.

CASE STUDY: STAFFING EXPERT
SAYS PERSONALIZATION IS KEY
FOR JOB SEEKERS

Donna Fitzgerald,
Owner and CEO of Contemporaries, Inc.
55 Ct. St., Ste 330, Boston, MA 02108
www.bostoncontemporaries.com
info@bostoncontemporaries.com
Phone (617) 723-9797
Fax (617) 723-4140

Attracting candidates has never been easier for staffing firms, such as Contemporaries, Inc., of Boston, Massachusetts. As a result of our Web site and the positive reviews our candidates post on sites like Citysearch, we are constantly garnering the attention of tech-savvy applicants. The question now, however, is how do we filter through all of the résumés we receive on any given day? This is particularly important considering the fact that many of the résumés and virtual job candidates look quite similar in terms of experience and skills.

There are several ways to get past this filter. First, do not make the types of mistakes that will lead to an automatic discarding or disqualification of your résumé. One example of this type of error, which occurs frequently with the rise in technology, is attaching a résumé without a cover letter, or a shortened version of a cover letter in the body of an e-mail. A cover letter is not always necessary; however, it is essential for a candidate to say something in the e-mail referencing the fact he or she is sending a résumé. Not taking this extra step comes across as impersonal. It is essential to make a connection with the e-mail recipient, given how impersonal the Internet itself is.

There are several ways that candidates can impress me immediately. Aside from being positive, it is imperative that the person's résumé is active, and that they seek out new challenges. I am also impressed by a candidate who shows me they have good problem-solving skills. No matter what the job is, if a person is a good problem-solver, then he or she will be that much better at a given job. It is also important that candidates' work ethic comes through. They can convey this through their e-mail by demonstrating commitment to jobs and their willingness to do the work to get

get the job. There is a fine line between being assertive and aggressive; the former is what an applicant should always aim to achieve. I want to feel like the candidate wants the job.

Along this vein, desperation does not come across well, either. Do not write "I have been looking for a job for several months and I need a job." Instead, demonstrate your flexibility and willingness to try new things you might not have done before — not because you are desperate, but because you like the challenge.

What Companies Look for in an Internet Résumé or Cover Letter

Companies are always on the hunt for the best candidate for their dollars. Turnover is expensive and stressful to other works, and especially to company managers because the employer has already invested time, money, and energy into hiring and training an employee who subsequently leaves the position. The company, in turn, has to rehire, and the process starts all over again.

When you stop to consider the administrative costs of bringing someone on board, there is usually a lot of hours spent ensuring the original candidate is properly trained, and that their paperwork is in order. Usually, there is also time devoted to giving equal consideration to the rest of the staff. When a person just does not work out, a business must replace him or her, or the employee's workload is handed off to fellow workers. Then, the rest of the employees are struggling with extra work, setting back the entire company.

Thus, employers go to great lengths to make sure the right choice is made when hiring a job candidate. A résumé or cover letter filled with misspellings, grammatical errors, and other mistakes is sure to catch the eye of a human resources representative or direct employer. They understand that the person probably will not work out if the candidate is too relaxed or unknowledgeable in his or her first interaction with a potential employer. Of course, the application may never go further than the submission stage.

A candidate who knows the language of the industry, on the other hand, can put together a powerful and concise cover letter that will catch the eye of the decision maker. In addition to paying attention to all of the details, such as spelling and grammar, the job candidate must able be able to convey why he or she is the perfect person for the position. Companies are primarily concerned with their own bottom lines — not the fact that the job would be perfect for a particular candidate, or that the person applying really just needs a break to get back into the job market.

As for the résumé, again, emphasize the tasks and responsibilities that you successfully accomplished, which are part of the position you are looking to be hired for. Take a good look at the job posting, and tweak your résumé to reflect and accentuate those areas of expertise. Say, for example, there is a great opening for a mid-level project manager's spot. While you may have served as both a project coordinator and a scheduler, rather than list every aspect of each job separately, you will want to work your résumé to reflect the job responsibilities and duties that were relative to project management. No matter how good you may have been at some of the other tasks, you will want to really hone in on the data that would make you a superior project manager, particularly because of the dual roles you held.

Unless an advertisement says "willing to train," most employers want a candidate who can hit the ground running once hired. Of course, there is a learning curve with any new position, but employers want to know that the person they select has the capabilities to not just do the job, but to do the job well. Companies usually know what they want from a job candidate and what skills are needed to be able to perform a job. That is why they go to great lengths to compose the advertisement with all the tasks, responsibilities, and skill levels necessary to succeed.

How Companies Determine Which Candidates to Call

It is difficult to provide a standard answer as to how companies decide who will and will not be called in for an interview. But there is always a group of applicants who will not make the cut. Think about how you make your own decisions. Sometimes you know what you want based on the process of elimination. If you have tried things in the past that did not work out, you may not be so quick to select the same product or service next time around.

The decision making process for a company is often similar to this. For example, a company may have found in the past that an individual who actually has an MBA works out well. The company's past employee, on the other hand, who was trying to juggle work and school, may not have left such a good impression — even though the employee was working toward an MBA. In a case like that, companies, too, will rely on their instincts and previous experiences. There are, however, some steps you can take to improve your chances of getting noticed, and possibly hired.

 Job Tip!

Employers are searching for the candidate who will be perfect for them and their company. Keep this in mind when composing your letter.

What keywords and phrases did you use?

Begin with your own job tools. Think about the language and whether or not your material conveys, even verbatim, the language used in the job posting, as well as standardized industry language.

Before even responding or applying to a job posting, make sure that you have the credentials and skills to be able to complete the tasks. Be prepared to back up your words with testing, references, and even samples of your work. You want to be able to show your potential employer the knowledge and skills you have, proving that you will be a valuable asset to the company.

There are certain words and phrases you should include in your résumé and cover letter to at least make it through the first hurdle when it comes to applying for a position.

For example, if you are going to a sales position, you may want to think about incorporating words and phrases like "call preparation," "sales productivity," or "customer relationship management (CRM)."

If some of the phrases and keywords you find in a job ad or Internet search about the industry do not mean anything to you, then try to avoid using them yourself until you do understand them. You just want to make sure that the keywords and phrases you do use are standard for the industry and that you do know their meaning and significance.

You will want to read the ad over a few times to determine where the keywords are placed, if there are tasks that seem like the same duty but phrased slightly different. Find out if any of the words or phrases are repeated in the job description within the duties and responsibilities as well as the requirements. Those are usually the areas where the company is placing the most emphasis, and the things they are looking for in an employee the most. Some companies use software programs to weed out candidates who do not have the right experience based on the job description or posting. It is important to find out which words will be used for this process. You should review an advertisement and look to see which words are repeated or emphasized. Many times, these are the keywords in the job ad.

Overall, what you include will depend on the jobs you are applying for. You may want to include keywords or phrases, in addition to other information, that shows your employer that you will be able to accomplish the tasks and responsibilities that the job requires, in addition to showing that you know your way around the industry and the profession.

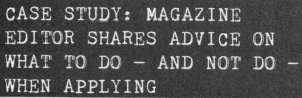

CASE STUDY: MAGAZINE
EDITOR SHARES ADVICE ON
WHAT TO DO – AND NOT DO –
WHEN APPLYING

Randy Lankford, managing editor
Scene in S.A. magazine
www.mysaweekly.com
900 NE Loop 410, Suite D-430
San Antonio, TX 78209
me@scenepublications.com

If you are going to work for Randy Lankford, who has been in the writing and publishing industry for some 35 years, you will need to be good at your profession — as well as Internet-savvy. Lankford uses the Internet as his exclusive means of finding and hiring his magazine staff.

"All my job candidates come from the Internet," Lankford said. "I am looking for employees who can not only put one word behind another, but have the technical savvy to interact online. If you can't find and respond to an online job ad, then you're probably not the person I'm looking for."

As a result of the number of résumés Lankford receives from online applicants, and the ease in which these candidates can apply, Lankford can afford to be "choosey" with who he entertains as possible candidates and who will not be given consideration.

"It's made me pickier," he said. "When you need to weed through a dozen résumés, it's easier if you throw out the ones that are poorly typed or formatted."

While he has seen his share of unqualified would-be writers, Lankford said that it does not stop there — cover letter and thank-you notes can be double-edged swords if there are mistakes. The managing editor said cover letters with typos or poor grammar are killers. Other red flags Lankford looks for are résumés and cover letters with incorrectly used keywords and phrases.

"If the writer is obviously trying to show off their vocabulary or ability to construct a convoluted sentence, I tend to shy away," said Lankford.

Using keywords can have a positive impact, though. Someone who knows about the industry he or she is applying to will be able to throw in some occasional jargon and use it correctly, letting Lankford and other employers know that the applicant has knowledge about the job he or she is applying for.

As an editor, Lankford is always short on time, so applicants who take extra steps to include items like portfolios and clips stand out.

"Make yourself easy to hire; cut to the chase and list your clips," he said. "Make them available online. I'm much more likely to respond to an application with clips, or better yet, links to clips, attached. Put a link to your e-mail in your letter or résumé so I can contact you immediately."

Finding Out What Makes You a Good Fit For the Company

Being a good fit for a particular company is much more than just being capable of performing the tasks and responsibilities included in a job description. A good fit is having the ability to work with a team of people. A good fit is being able to adapt to a work environment and get along with coworkers and managers. A good fit will help the company's success overall. A bad fit, on the other hand, is noticeable and brings stress to the workplace. Both the candidate and the employer will succeed — or, to some extent, fail — if the fit is not right.

 Job Tip!

If you are starting with a staffing agency, ask if they have a group of clients, or whether they would want you to contact them if you find a job possibility. Some companies feel more comfortable going through a staffing agency before making a permanent hire. Employers, through the temp-to-hire program, get to try a candidate out before signing him or her out permanently. The employer will use the staffing agency to first screen candidates to make sure their credentials are in order and they are a good fit for the position. Then, if the employee performs well, the company may choose to permanently hire them after the temporary period is over.

For example, if you have spent most of your career in a governmental work setting and you are applying to a company that is very laidback and does not have any set rules, neither you nor your potential employer may be happy with the fit. If you are used to regimented routines, taking orders, and dressing up in a uniform or your best business professional suits, you may not adapt very well in a company environment free with creative thought that is relaxed with their rules. Unless you can be a chameleon in the work force, you may be setting yourself up for failure.

Because of the work style you are used to, you may have a difficult time getting your foot through the door. Despite the fact that your credentials from your former job in the government are impeccable, they are not what the freestyle, creative company is looking for in their group of workers.

While you may not have the final say as to whether or not an employer determines that you are the right fit or not, there are steps you can take to try and increase the odds in your favor.

Why Your Résumé Gets Lost in the Pile

The presentation a candidate makes to a seasoned recruiter or a human resources representative tells much more than you would think. For instance, a candidate who submits a lengthy résumé and cover letter is not always seen as an overachiever, or as someone who is eager for the job, or who has a lot of experience. To a recruiter, it is sometimes the equivalent of getting cornered at a social or family function by the person other guests try to avoid. It is the person who will spend the next 15 minutes rambling on about him or herself, including many more details than you care to know. Receiving a résumé and cover letter that is excessive, in which the information could have been conveyed in a page or two, is like receiving a visit from an unwelcomed guest — except in this case, the recruiter is not forced to spend 15 minutes on the person. The recruiter may immediately place the paperwork in the undesirable pile he or she has created for those who will not be hired. If the recruiter does decide to go over each point of your résumé, you are certainly not ingratiating yourself with him or her from the start.

Staffing agencies want to see a résumé that indicates professionalism. A résumé that is worded correctly, including grammar and punctuation, and right to the point is one way to garner attention. Even staffing agencies, to some degree, have become a niche business. While there are still agencies that cater to all jobs and all candidates, more and more agencies specialize in particular industry or field. Say, for example, you are looking to get into the medical profession; you would not send your résumé to an agency that specializes in general labor or accounting. Make your audience known, and send your résumé to an appropriate agency that deals with positions in your field.

How well do you follow directions?

There is a great deal that employers, recruiters, and HR staff members can tell from an online application, the first being whether a candidate can navigate through the Internet and whether they can follow directions or are willing to take the time to fill out an application. For example, if the application process asks the candidate to submit an application, and then to submit their résumé in text document form rather than a designed résumé in Word, the recruiter will know right away if the candidate is up to the task. Candidates who disregard the instructions may just use the original form of their résumé. The only problem is that the document will not arrive in the same form as these candidates expected — the form that it is in on their computers. Sometimes, when you try to copy and paste information from one document into another program, it will look different, visually. If your résumé happens to have bulleted lists, the bullets may end up transforming into question marks if the programs are different. The recruiter is going to know right away that you either were unable to do the specified task, or that you did not want to follow the directions.

Errors in sending or receiving your résumé

In other cases, you may be asked to upload your résumé at the beginning of the online application process. After that, you may decide that you do not want to spend the next 20 or 30 minutes filling in the blanks for all the information contained in your résumé. By doing this, you could create technical problems that would eliminate you from the pool of applicants.

Some companies allow for the uploading of résumés, although their own computer programs only capture the contact information. They do not have access to the actual résumé. Therefore, if you decide not to complete the rest of your application — assuming that the recruiter will have the information he or she needs from your résumé — you could actually be taking yourself out of the race for the job. Without filling out the entire online application, the company may not have a way of having your work history and a record of your skills. Because of the way they recruit, some companies will not be able to tell a lot just from an uploaded résumé.

If you upload your résumé to a job application of a company who can download things in their entirety, there still may be obstacles to face before actually getting your résumé into the hands of the decision-maker. For example, your résumé may be directed to one department while the online application is actually the first level of screening in determining whose résumés will be reviewed and which ones will be eliminated from the selection process. As an applicant, you will never know where your résumé really goes. However, if you do not fill out the online application, chances are the recruiter or HR staff member is not going to call. By not filling out the application, you have exhibited the fact that you are unwilling to follow direction, or that you will not put in the necessary effort to even throw your name into the hat. Either way, you, as a job seeker, will lose out.

You may want to submit your documents as PDF files, thereby eliminating the possibility that they will be altered in any way. In order for you to create such a file, you will need to purchase a product such as Adobe Acrobat. The Adobe Reader — which allows you to read PDF files — is a free download. Once you have your document prepared, then with little effort you can convert it to a PDF file and upload it to your e-mails or job profiles in this form. As long as the receiver has the Reader capacity, they will be able to access your document, open, and read it. To create a PDF of your résumé in Microsoft Word:

1. Go to the "File" menu and select "Save as."
2. Enter in the name of the document you are saving.
3. Click on the "Format" tab to change the way the Word document is saved.
4. Select "PDF."
5. Click "Save."

Do you really meet the criteria?

Job seekers and employers, for the most part, have a common goal: to find a job and a candidate who is going to succeed in the position. Often times, job seekers will go ahead and apply for a position they may have some of the skills or experience for, or a job that they merely would like to have.

Knowing when not to apply

There may have been a point in time when a job candidate could be partially right for a position, having half the skills or experience needed to do the job, and would still be hired. But as the number of job candidates in the market increases, only those individuals with the essential skills, credentials, and experience will be called and hired.

And while you may find lucrative job postings you would like to apply for — because the money is so good or the location is within walking distance from your home — you are better off passing on the interview if you are not qualified.

Applying for jobs you are unqualified for wastes your time, as well as the time of an employer or hiring manager. Plus, if a position opens up later in the company that you are qualified for, chances are you will not get called because the same hiring manager, who already processed your résumé, may not take your candidacy seriously and may think you are just randomly applying to any and all job listings.

Passing security clearance

Another reason your job application may seem to get lost in a stack of résumés is because you have not passed a **security clearance**. This will not be required for all jobs, but for many government agencies and companies that work with children — including schools — criminal background checks, credit background checks, and drug testing are becoming standard pre-qualification methods.

A security clearance is a standing or status, issued by the military and government, allowing the individual to access various levels of information, as it pertains to a particular job. The process for receiving a security clearance is usually lengthy and involves a more in-depth background check than what is required by most employers. The process includes all of the information gathered through the criminal and credit background review, but may go much deeper into a person's background, personal, and professional history. It may also include a polygraph test to be taken by the candidate.

There are various levels of security clearances, from national agency clearances (NAC), to Secret and Top-Secret clearances. You will know if you have clearance because you will be asked to fill out a substantial amount of information that will be checked and verified. You will be asked permission before a company, government, or military entity begins the process. But, if you are thinking about pursuing a career in an organization that deals with sensitive information, plan on answering yes to an extensive background check. There are job sites, such as **www.clearancejobs.com**, that are dedicated to this niche. The jobs may range from military marketing specialist, to engineer, to IT systems analyst, or even sales director. The reason why you need such clearance may be the work you will be doing, or even where you will be working from. One final note: You will not be able to receive your own security clearance in anticipation of a job search. There is a formal process that has to be followed. Usually only companies with government and military contracts, or government agencies or military branches themselves, can ask to initiate the process if they are planning on hiring an individual.

 Job Tip!

Honesty is the best policy. When you sign documents indicating that you agree to a background security investigation, there are very few personal records that are off-limits to the investigator. Having a traffic ticket or a bankruptcy may not prevent you from securing a job, but being dishonest during your security clearance investigation may cost you a job. A lot of times, investigators already know the answers to the questions they may be asking you.

CASE STUDY: EXECUTIVE
RECRUITER EXPLAINS WHICH
CANDIDATES WILL BE CALLED
AND SEEN

Hassan Shariff,
Executive Recruiter,
MetLife Insurance Co.
Long Island City, NY

Qualified candidates with the right job skills, credentials, experience, and outstanding written communication skills are the contenders who catch the eye of Executive Recruiter Hassan Shariff, of MetLife in New York. The recruiter said an average of 90 to 95 percent of applicants are not qualified for the job posting they apply for.

Where do these unsuitable candidates come from? The answer, according to Shariff, is simple.

"Roughly 80 percent of the job candidates are leverage through the Internet," he said.

To employers, receiving applications from candidates who do not have the necessary skills sets is not seen as ambitious; it is seen as a waste of time, and portrays the applicant in bad light.

"It shows that they didn't read the job posting," Shariff said.

Plus, some companies, like MetLife, use a job candidate tracking system, which logs all of the job openings for which an applicant applied. When applicants apply to more than one position within a company, it makes it often evident that they are just in search of a job — any job — and will not necessarily be a fit for any of the positions because the required experience is lacking.

MetLife®

If you are taking the time to conduct a thoughtful job search, make sure you follow the rules of the game when it comes to applying for positions.

Have all of your tools at the ready, and make sure to search and apply for jobs you are truly qualified for — not ones you would just like to try out. Be sure to incorporate keywords and key phrases in your résumé and cover letters for the specific job you are applying for. Whether you are dealing with a staffing agency or a company, make sure to follow through with a thank-you e-mail whenever possible. Personalize the experience and let employers know why you are not only qualified for the job you are applying for, but that you are the best candidate for the job.

If you follow these rules, you will greatly increase your chances of being called in for an interview. Your chances for getting hired will also increase, as long as you are willing to put in the time and the effort, and approach the process in a professional manner.

CHAPTER 8

Setting Yourself Apart From the Internet Applicant Pack

Internet Lingo

Blog: A Web site used to post messages, comments, opinions, or whole conversations. A business entity or individual can own a particular blog, which they maintain and provide content for on a regular basis.

Domain name: The name that identifies an Internet address. This is the first part of an URL. For example, in the Web address www.choosinganame.com/index.html, the domain name is choosinganame.com.

Friendships or friending: A means to form virtual relationships through the use of the Internet. These relationships may be with people you already know, or others whom you may come in contact with through the Internet.

Internet profile: A virtual portrait someone creates of themselves by answering questions and entering information. The profile can read like a résumé, but can also include photographs and other documents. A profile can be filled with personal and professional information, or a combination of both.

Photo sharing sites: Sites where you can go to upload your photographs, edit them, and send them to others. Sites include Flickr (**www.flickr.com**) and Photobucket (**http://photobucket.com**).

Privacy setting: A means to set the settings on your computer or your e-mail to control the types of information that will be allowed to go into your computer, as well as activities such as unauthorized changes to your computer, or the prevention of various tracking cookies into the computer.

Tweeting: A form of communication used by people who belong to the social network Twitter, **http://twitter.com**. The free social networking site allows you to follow other people or groups as you post your own messages for others to keep in touch and respond. There is a maximum of 140 characters to each message, which equals approximately 40 words per message.

Web host: A company or organization that provides space on their server for Internet users to create their own Web sites. These companies also provide connectivity to the Internet.

On a daily basis, for any given job, employers may find themselves with anywhere from 25 to a hundred résumés. After a while, most of the paperwork may look very much the same like vanilla ice cream — same white paper, same black print, same style, and even the same experience and credentials.

While the hiring entity may really like vanilla ice cream, they may also want to delve into some of the other flavors as well. Through the use of the Internet, you can offer a potential employer something more unique.

If you are willing to put in the time and the effort, you can set yourself apart from the rest of the Internet job candidates and come out on top. But again, it will take effort and planning, and you will have to follow-through. At the end of it all, a brand-new job with a brand-new salary may be the best reward for all your efforts.

With all of the available tools at your disposal, it is merely a matter of learning how to set yourself apart and implementing the necessary changes to dazzle someone who has never laid eyes on you.

CASE STUDY: HELPING PEOPLE THROUGH THE JOB SEARCH PROCESS

Terry Starr,
Co-founder of MyWorkButterfly.com
Parsippany, NJ

Terry Starr, along with her partner Bradi Nathan, created **http://My-WorkButterfly.com** as a means to help other moms — some who were stay-at home moms, and others who were working. Their dream was to create the most comprehensive social network of its kind.

The site was originally designed to provide support, advice, and entertainment for other mothers. "We provide free resources with 24/7 access to jobseekers," Starr said.

Starr said when they polled their group of users — mainly mothers — she and her partner found that jobs, or job-related material, was the No. 1 thing their site's visitors and users wanted. The participants wanted the information through a social network.

In addition to some of the standard items you would find on a job board, such as job postings, Starr's site also includes other job-related support items, such as a Career Coach and Psychotherapist. Additionally, their articles not only focus on topics such as interviewing and returning to the work force, but also deal with other material such as childcare, working mother's guilt, parenting, fitness, and nutrition. The site also features celebrity mothers, lifestyle articles, and celebrity and entertainment news.

Starr, who spent some 30 years in the recruitment advertising industry, pointed out that the site is a great starting point for mothers who have been out of the workforce and are looking to return, as well as for working mothers who have many of the same issues as their non-parenting colleagues.

Starr praised the virtues of social networking, explaining the many values such virtual communities hold.

"A social network like ours is huge. Knowing there is a place where you can go and get advice, support, and solutions, absolutely free, is very appealing," Starr said.

She wanted her site to convey the fact that there are others who can relate to the stress working mothers endure, as a way of telling them they are not alone. "There are experts and like-minded women waiting to connect with you," Starr said to her large Web audience.

"In addition to offering employers job postings, we also provide other ways for them to communicate directly with our moms within the network. Right now, we are finalizing proposals for some major global companies who are specifically targeting the 'return-to-the-workforce' mom."

Unlike other job boards and job sites, Starr's Web site, which has its own job board, is also designed as a means of personalizing the Internet experience by encouraging visitors and users to develop friendships.

"Remember that anything you write in any of these social networking communities are also available to recruiters who are absolutely checking your social networking pages. So beware," she concluded.

MYWORKBUTTERFLY.COM
FOR MOMS WHO WANT TO SPREAD THEIR WINGS

Invent — and Reinvent — Yourself Online

The beauty of the Internet, particularly through profiles and networking, is that it allows job candidates to develop their personalities — both personally and professionally. You are in charge of your own profile, as it will reflect and emphasize only the information you want to draw attention to.

If you do not have any type of presence on the Internet, you can start by creating several profiles for various sites and social networks. Always keep in mind that if you are creating a profile for personal or business purposes, many people, including potential employers, can easily access your information. In fact, according to a 2009 survey done by CareerBuilder, 45 percent of employers interviewed said that they used social networks to research their job candidates. The percentage more than doubled from 2008, when only 22 percent of employers said they were using the sites as an additional candidate-screening tool.

It should also be pointed out that sites like Facebook®, MySpace®, and Twitter™, all mentioned later in this chapter, also allow you to control how public you want your information to be. The controls allow you to decide who will be able to access your information. You just need to read through the instructions on how to manage your personal security settings for the sites. Remember, it will do you no good to showcase yourself as the right job candidate if your Internet profile is weak or unprofessional. This is not the time to be modest; rather, it is the time to sing your own praises, accentuate your major accomplishments, and provide viewers with a glimpse of who you are.

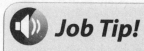 *Job Tip!*

Reinventing yourself as an expert, if you do in fact have the credentials, is just one way to catch the eye of a potential employer.

Be as honest as possible when posting information pertaining to your career and work experience. Remember, not only will potential employers potentially be able to view your information, but previous employers and fellow co-workers could, as well.

The online presence that you are developing should be one that you are proud of, and one that you are more than willing to show off to a potential employer. While you may have beaten out many others and secured an interview, you will only be allotted a certain amount of time in a face-to-face interview with an employer or a recruiter. With the right Internet presence, you can go a little further in showing your potential employers what you are made of and what you are capable of. You can invite them to view your site. Once there, you have again shown that you are a cut above the rest, as long as your material is fresh, professional, and relevant.

The fact the Internet and Web sites still present an element of the unknown provides you with a perfect opportunity to really floor someone with your professional knowledge and presence. This will work particularly well if you take the time to develop a site that is extremely professional and balanced. It is the kind of opportunity that may push you into hiring status if you come out of an interview neck and neck with another qualified individual. It is your opportunity to provide a potential employer with a glimpse into the many untapped talents and resources you possess but were not able to display during a canned interview session.

Creating Your Internet Profile

Having an **Internet profile** can be very lucrative when you stop to consider the fact it is like having free advertisements all about you. Sometimes employers like to see what qualities a job candidate has before making any formal contact. This is where a job seeker can sink or swim, especially if there is no profile.

On many job sites, you can create a professional Internet profile without using any of the available social networking sites, like Facebook, MySpace, and LinkedIn. On some larger sites, a great deal of the information is compiled, like a template, and you only need to fill in the blanks. Other sites have no templates.

These online profiles, as created within the job site you are using to search for open positions, make it easy for employers to locate all your information, and allow them to quickly learn a little more about you than what is generally included in your résumé and cover letter. Keep in mind that even if you develop a profile using a job search site, you may still want to create a social networking profile, too.

You may want to create multiple profiles of yourself to show the many sides to your endless talents and skills. Accentuate the good and include information relevant to a particular career path you want to take. For example, if you are looking to get into finance, you may want to create one profile emphasizing any banking, accounting, or financial planning experience you have. You may want to create another profile highlighting your business development experience, your entrepreneurial spirit, as well as your credentials and accomplishments. This is not the time to mention any failed business ventures. You do not have to include every single aspect of your life, but rather only those items that will enhance your image and give potential employers a glimpse into the types of skills and experiences you could bring to their company.

Developing your character online

To start creating your virtual brand, it may be wise to have all the information handy. You may want to write everything down first in a notebook, or just have your résumé nearby. You will want to include information about your skills, work experience, awards, commendations, certifications, professional organizations, and education. Because you have assembled all the information ahead of time, you will save yourself endless hours of retracing your steps or locating the information. This way, should you decide to create more than one profile, the data will be right at your fingertips.

Depending on which site, or sites, you use, you may be prompted to fill in fields, listing relevant information, or you may have the option of being able to use a document stored in your computer, simply copying and pasting the date right into the profile. Other profiles may direct you to select a career path, or may have a built-in mechanism that helps you determine the steps you need to take in order to fulfill your job or career goal. The site may require you to use keywords that describe your work or your personality. All of these factors go into developing your presence online.

Keep in mind that many job search Web sites, such as CareerBuilder.com and Monster.com, allow you to build your profiles on their own site, much like you upload your résumé and cover letter. This way, you are covering all of your bases with potential employers, business professionals, or recruiters, looking for someone with your particular talents and skills. Your information will be stored on the site, and often, it is best to do this when you first register for an account. *For more information about choosing a job search engine or site, see Chapter 3.*

Once your profile is created and stored, you can complete the entire application process in less than a minute, if you wanted to.

1) Start off by signing into the site.

2) Find the right job listing and click the "Apply Now" button. Another screen will pop up, saying "Apply for this job."

3) There will be two boxes for your name and your e-mail address. Directly under that, a box to upload your résumé will also appear.

4) At the bottom of the page it will also give you the option to "Include cover letter." You can check yes or leave it blank.

5) Once you type in your name and e-mail address, and upload your résumé and cover letter, you can click "Send Application."

6) You will receive a thank-you message for applying, along with a note that you have just finished applying for the position. It will also provide you with the job title and company in which you have just applied.

It took you years to get where you are today, which is why you should take the time to fill out these profiles — give your employers a glimpse of the person you have worked to be. And if you are just starting out, your willingness to learn and your ability to go the distance will also provide would-be employers with a glimpse into the type of employee you would make. Putting together a professional profile is going to again take time and effort. When filling out information for your profile, remember to stay as professional as possible. You do not have to mention every little aspect of your life; just stick to the relevant facts as they pertain to your future career.

Filling in the profile

Start with posting your profiles on the bigger, more popular sites, such as Monster.com, CareerBuilder.com, and Yahoo! HotJobs. The questions, for the most part, are basically the same, although there will be some additional information that can be added depending on the specific site you post your profile on. An important point to remember is that potential employers will be viewing your profile, if you choose to make it public. Again, you may want to stick to the more pertinent points of your professional life when creating your profile. There may be a place to list your interests and hobbies, like line-dancing, joke-telling, juggling, or horseshoe throwing, but it may not be the wisest idea to list them as high points in your professional Internet profile.

Navigate to one of the sites mentioned, like Monster.com or Careerbuilder. com. Once you register, you can create a profile for yourself. Most profiles will require the individual to answer basic questions about themselves.

A basic profile questionnaire may look something like this:

Sample Profile Questionnaire

Contact Information
Name:
Address:
Home Phone:
Cell Phone:
E-mail Address:

Mission or Career Objective
Statement:

Work Experience
Job titles, dates, companies, duties, and responsibilities

Education
Schools attended, years, diploma, degree, other

Certifications
Professional certifications and dates they were obtained

Skills
Computer skills, other job- or industry-related competencies

Honors or awards
Honors, awards, or accomplishments

Memberships
Professional memberships to groups and organizations

The finished profile may look something like this:

Profile

Jane Smith
123 Walkway Park, Seattle, WA
555-123-457 or
555-987-654
j.smith10@domain.com

Mission or Career Objective
To find a position as a Business Analyst, where my experience and skills in basic financial analysis, and my keen ability to uncover new business prospects and identify cost-savings opportunities, will be fully maximized.

Most Recent Work Experience
2006 - Present - Business Analyst for XYZ Company, Seattle, Washington

Responsibilities
- Provide expert analysis to top executive level management staff

- Uncover financial opportunities for the company, which to date, has led to a $500,000 increase in bottom-line profit margins

- Identify areas where cost savings could be realized, resulting in a $270,000 reduction in professional and operational services

Education
MBA from the University of Washington

Certifications
BA – Certified from B2B, Online course
Six Sigma – Certified as a Black Belt, Online course

Skills
MS Office Suite – Highly proficient: 5-7 years' experience
Internet Explorer – Highly proficient: 5-7 years' experience
Internet Outlook – Highly proficient: 5-7 years' experience
Data Analysis Tools – Advanced: 3-5 years' experience
SQL (Structured Query Language) – Advanced: 3-5 years' experience

Honors or awards
Graduated with honors in the top 10% from University of Washington;
Received five awards from previous employer for outstanding analysis
and service

Memberships
Society of American Business Analysts (SABA)

Profiles can be lengthy, but are usually shorter than a résumé because they provide a summary of the person's professional, and sometimes personal, experiences. In other instances the profile will include a short summary along with the individual's résumé.

CASE STUDY: JOB CANDIDATE FOUND MAXIMIZING INTERNET PRESENCE PAYS OFF IN JOB SEARCH

Morgan Moran
Chandler, AZ
http://morganmoran.com

Through the Internet you can create your own presence, and sometimes that is exactly what you need to set yourself ahead of other job contenders. Morgan Moran, interactive search and social media marketing consultant, started his quest for a new job by doing just that.

After developing his tools, such as his résumés and cover letters, and registering on many of the large job sites, Moran found that he had very little presence on the Internet, despite the fact he had spent nearly a dozen years working in such fields as Internet marketing and social media networking. It was time to expand his set of tools.

"I purchased the domain name morganmoran.com and built a simple Web site with my personal background, my professional experience, and a little about my family," Moran said. "I also started a blog for posting ideas related to my industry and created a social media hub where people can find links to all of my professional networking profiles, pictures I posted to **Flickr**, a feed of all of my recent Twitter posts, and a feed of all of my recent blog posts."

His efforts did not stop there. "I [would] then check on the professional networking sites to see if anyone in my network knows anyone at that company and ask them to introduce me."

Moran, who holds a bachelor's degree in business/marketing, used the Internet and social networking sites to brand and market himself to employers. He followed the advice of any good advertising agent — get your name out there and garner visibility. By doing this online, he directed potential employers to focus on his abilities as an interactive marketing manager, which he said was vital to his job search and procurement.

"The idea is to get yourself out there so that anyone, anywhere can find you," he said.

Social Networking

Think of social networking as the cliques and groups of students in high school, or as the people who would sit together at lunch in your old company. Social networking, however, has taken on a new face, even though it works in essentially the same manner — just with more possibilities.

Social networking and other forms of communication began as a means for people to use the Internet to stay in touch with friends, make new acquaintances, and socialize with others. Whether they were a group of classmates, people who shared similar interests, or neighborhood pals or relatives, you could catch up on the latest gossip. Today, you can also present yourself in a way you have always aspired to be seen by peers and potential bosses — as long as you distinguish your professional life from your personal life.

Internet profiles using social networks are also becoming more and more popular. Thousands upon thousands of such profiles can be found on blogs, or on sites such as LinkedIn^{SM}, MySpace® and Facebook®. Remember that the Internet is generally a very public place, and you will have no way of knowing who is looking at your profile. However, there are ways of allowing a select few to view all of your personal pages. Sites like MySpace® can be set so that only people you know and approve will be able to see all of your material, such as quotes, pictures, and other friends. But, for the purposes of a professional profile, you will most likely want to keep your **privacy setting** on public to ensure accessibility for your potential employers.

While you are creating a public summary of yourself, and trying to decide what to include or not to include, ask yourself whether the material is something you would want a potential employer to view. You have no way of knowing whether the material you post will be seen by someone who could be your next employer or work colleague. When you are thinking in these terms, you must think about your professional profile, as well as your personal profile.

Professional versus personal

There are no real right or wrong answers when it comes to determining whether you will use social networking sites for either professional or personal use, or a combination of the two. Keep in mind, however, that if you are on the job and decide to make a personalized appearance on one of the social networks, you may want to keep it set on a setting that only allows your invited friends, guests, and acquaintances to access. The opportunities for personalization are so tempting that you may not want to pass up a venue that allows you to connect with old classmates or friends. But always exercise caution when deciding who will have access to your profile — you never know who will be looking at it.

By the same token, if you decide to make a professional appearance, everything on your site should be professional. That means:

- No misspellings
- No pictures that are not aligned properly
- No sloppy work or amateur design
- No talk of last week's party
- No office gossip
- No unprofessional content

Remember, you will not be able to see someone's reaction to your work, so you should strive to impress your online acquaintances. You may feel the impact of your professional profiles when you do not receive any calls or e-mails about professional jobs from your professional social networking.

Billing yourself as the class clown or best partier are not the types of publicly displayed information that will influence a potential employer in any kind of favorable light. So, unless you are vying to become a comedian or a fraternity member straight out of *Animal House*, keep the unprofessional material out of your professional profile.

There is, of course, the option of having the best of both worlds, where some of your Internet presence is designed for personal use, while another part of your presence is designed for professional use. That way, you can keep each group separate. You may want to use your Twitter or LinkedIn account only for professional purposes, while you may want to have another profile on MySpace used for social entertainment. Just watch your settings for both sites. Additionally, you may want to have two separate e-mail addresses — one affiliated with your professional life and another to address your personal needs.

Blogs

Starting a **blog** can be an eye-catching way to show an employer that you are knowledgeable on a subject, and that you can speak eloquently about it. A blog is a personalized page, log, or presentation that a user can create, post on the Internet, and share with other people. The content can be updated or changed sometimes daily, weekly, or monthly, but usually has to do with topics that are related to your industry, or that your potential employer will view as interesting or important. You may also think about partnering with a photographer who would like to get their work exhibited through the Internet. They could take pictures for your blog, as long as you provide the subject matter. You can include images, links, video, and written content on your blog, all of which can express your opinion or can be informative in nature. Regardless of what your blog is about, your goal is to catch your employer's eye.

If you are looking to get into an environmentally friendly "green" job, you may want to consider starting a blog where you will talk about environmental issues. You may want to also want to consider being a contributor to a Web site. As a contributor, you can address various subjects in your field or expertise. If your career ambition is in the field of photography, what better way to let a potential employers know how talented you are than by being able to have them see for themselves through a personalized Web site full of your photographs?

To create a blog, go to a site that offers free blogging and register. WordPress. com (**http://wordpress.com**), Blogger (**www.blogger.com**), and LiveJournal (**www.livejournal.com**) are just some of the sites. Most of these sites also include templates to help you with the process and teach you how to create a visually appealing blog. You may get a following of readers through your blog, which could increase your chance of getting job leads. If you are running for a position, having a blog about a particular service, product, or other relevant item may be just what you need to push you ahead of your Internet competitors.

If you decide to use your blog in a professional manner, you can blog about jobs and other related information. Not only can you refer your potential employers to your blog, but you can make valuable acquaintances who may be able to assist you in your journey to another job or another profession. The possibilities are endless. But if you want to blog about your cat, it may not be worth sharing with a potential employer.

Sample Blog: Tapping into Your Cre8ivity

Holly Marie Gibbs, graphic designer
E-mail: hollymariegibbs@yahoo.com
www.thecre8ive.blogspot.com
www.thecre8ive.com
www.hollymariegibbs.com
Twitter: @TheCre8ive

Holly Marie Gibbs stumbled across her love for graphic design in an unusual way.

As a freshman in high school, Gibbs enrolled in a journalism class with one of her friends. What she knew was that she would have a familiar face in class, but what she didn't know was how much she would enjoy it. In fact, she ended up being the co-editor of the newspaper.

Gibbs and the other editor would alternate the editorial and design respon-sibilities each month, trying to find a fair balance for the work they both wanted to do — design.

"We would fight over who used to do the design," Gibbs said.

Since high school, Gibbs started expanding her design experience with col-lege classes and summer journalism camps, where she always opted for the design courses. Now, the full-time designer uses her blog as an additional way to stay current in her field. The following blog posts are samples from her blog, followed by Gibbs' insight about the post.

the cre8ive

Search.

Home   Posts RSS   Comments RSS   Edit

Wednesday, August 12, 2009

The Cre8ive Interviews :: Ryan Deussing of Supermarket

Posted by Holly Marie Gibbs
8:04 AM

When I first ran across Supermarket, I couldn't help myself — I had to share what I had found. But posting about the site wasn't enough. I contacted Ryan Deussing of Brooklyn-based Supercorp, the development company behind the site, and asked him a few questions about what goes on behind the scenes.

TC: What inspired you to start Supermarket?

SM: We started Supermarket because we wanted to create an opportunity for designers and makers to sell their work within a carefully curated marketplace. Our aim was, and remains, to use or efforts to promote really fantastic design and help shoppers to discover great products.

TC: The site is such a thriving place for creatives. Is that something you feel was lacking before its conception?

SM: We love the fact that the talented designers at Supermarket attract others who want to follow suit and sell their own work. There's an element of community to the participating designers that we're really thrilled to watch develop.

TC: In your opinion, what is it about collaboration that works so well? In what ways do you think it is conducive to the creative process?

SM: I don't think you can make collaboration work, it's sort of like attraction. But when people who share similar passions discover each other, and find themselves working together and sharing ideas, that's when collaboration can really fuel great things.

TC: What is your favorite thing about Supermarket?

SM: It's really simple - I love seeing designers find success with their work, and I love watching people discover great products. When I see that someone in Sweden has just ordered something awesome from a designer in Chicago, I feel like we're succeeding.

TC: Where do you pull inspiration from? Who are some of your personal favorite creatives out there?

SM: I'm inspired by people who are following their passion and sharing it with others, whether they're making music, art, design, or food.

TC: What other projects are on the horizon for you? Anything that has you really pumped up?

SM: We have several things we're cooking up right now that will translate into a richer experience for shoppers and sellers at Supermarket. I can't actually name them, but we're eager to reveal them soon.

TC: Any advice for the masses — On life? On work? On starting a business?

SM: Don't try to keep up with the Joneses.

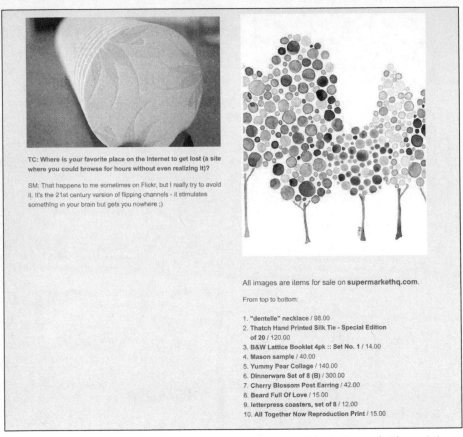

TC: Where is your favorite place on the Internet to get lost (a site where you could browse for hours without even realizing it)?

SM: That happens to me sometimes on Flickr, but I really try to avoid it. It's the 21st century version of flipping channels - it stimulates something in your brain but gets you nowhere ;)

All images are items for sale on **supermarkethq.com**.

From top to bottom:

1. "dentelle" necklace / 98.00
2. Thatch Hand Printed Silk Tie - Special Edition of 20 / 120.00
3. B&W Lattice Booklet 4pk :: Set No. 1 / 14.00
4. Mason sample / 40.00
5. Yummy Pear Collage / 140.00
6. Dinnerware Set of 8 (B) / 300.00
7. Cherry Blossom Post Earring / 42.00
8. Beard Full Of Love / 15.00
9. letterpress coasters, set of 8 / 12.00
10. All Together Now Reproduction Print / 15.00

Images and content of The Cre8ive used with permission

Why she blogged about it:

"I wanted to interview the team behind Supermarket as soon as I happened upon their Web site," Gibbs said. "I could tell just by poking around that they were a design-driven group, and I knew it would be fun to get some insight into their creative process, as well as the back story to their business. What really stuck out to me was that I could tell they cared about the designers who had stores with them just through their Web site. There is a certain magic there that says, 'We actually care.'"

Search.

Home   Posts RSS   Comments RSS   Edit

Thursday, June 11, 2009

Jewels of New York cupcakes

Posted by Holly Marie Gibbs
2:06 AM

Aren't these cupcakes the bee's knees? They're by **The Jewels of New York**, a fancy schmancy bakery that's always popping up with **brilliant creations**. They look like they come with little seed packets, which are very sweet. I've always wanted to eat a fancy cupcake but wonder if I could actually bite into something this beautiful. I didn't even realize they were edible at first glance. Now that's what I call edible art!

Images and content of The Cre8ive used with permission

Why she blogged about it:

"I chose to write a post about JONY simply because I thought their cupcakes and packaging were gorgeous," Gibbs said. "I'm (often) guilty of blogging about something for the sole reason that I think it's beautiful and should be shared. I find myself admiring and inspired by the work of all types of creatives who work in a variety of mediums and I love to share pretty things with my readers. I also really love that my posts create an archive of what is inspiring and catching my eye in a chronological way. It helps me to see how my tastes have evolved and developed over time."

Search.

Home   Posts RSS   Comments RSS   Edit

Thursday, June 18, 2009

Corporate Social Responsibility reports

Posted by Holly Marie Cibbs
9:29 AM

I do freelance graphic design work for a environmental communications and marketing **agency**, and one of our clients is **Anvil Knitwear, Inc.** [check out the **New For 2009 catalog**, that was one of the projects I designed for]. One of Anvil's main initiatives is to continue to develop and diversify their environmental and social responsibility efforts. Our job was to help showcase those efforts, so I spent a lot of time looking at the CSR reports from countless companies [CSR reports are a huge trend right now in the corporate world, and almost every major company publishes one]. While going through these reports, I noticed that a modular design scheme was definitely the way to go — these companies are trying to showcase all of their amazing efforts in one place and, as well all know, the world is rife with ADD-ridden people browsing the Web. One of my favorite sites and reports belonged to **Seventh Generation**, where colors and geometric shapes really helped to buy their readers' time.

Seventh Generation's Web site:

Seventh Generation's CSR report Web site:

Seventh Generation's CSR report:

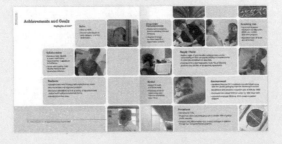

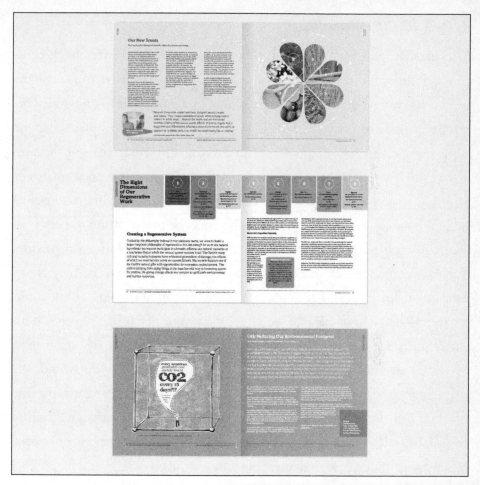

Images and content of The Cre8ive used with permission

Why she blogged about it:

"I chose to do a post about CSRs because I had been working on a report for a company I freelance for and was doing a lot of research on different ways to present the information," Gibbs said. "My favorite thing about this post was getting to talk about the projects I was working on in my life, while featuring the reports that influenced my design decisions. I like giving my readers a look into the process of design and showing them how an idea can grow through a little research and creative problem-solving."

Ways to communicate

Sites like MySpace®, ZooLoo™, Facebook®, and LinkedIn℠ present all kinds of possibilities for job seekers, professionally and personally. You can show how savvy you are about a topic or subject by your postings and added attractions exclusive to your particular web page. If you do not choose the right settings, just about anyone can view your information, and the sites also provide you with a perfect place to create a professional identity for yourself. In addition, they will also allow you access to members who may be in the same position as you are, or they may be in a position to help you. You will need to go onto the sites, register, and create your own **profile**. You may choose to have profiles on each site, especially because they are all free. If you are planning to use a site for professional reasons, think about what potential employers will see if they view your personalized page. With the templates some sites provide, you can decide what type of background or wallpaper you want to post, what picture of yourself you would like to include, and what type of information you would like to use the site for. You can also invite different individuals to link to your page, creating **friendships**. If you are planning on using any or all of the sites for personal reasons, just make sure that anything you post on it will be acceptable to a potential employer if, by chance, they somehow manage to find their way onto your site.

If you are planning on using your LinkedIn profile for professional reasons, design it accordingly, with information geared toward complete professionalism. That way, you can invite a potential employer to learn more about you by reading your site. With all of the networking Web sites available, there are many ways you can create a professional Internet presence — it is just a matter of finding out which platform is best for your needs.

A great feature for most of these sites includes the ability to chat, send messages, and most importantly, learn about the other person. In most of the sites, if you invite someone to connect with you, they will have an opportunity to learn what you are like from your virtual profile — and you will be given an opportunity to see what they are like from their profile.

MySpace is a social networking Web site that allows users to create a personalized visual presence on the Internet. You can post writings and upload photos, music, and videos to your own MySpace page. By signing up, users can have their own personal URL address, write blogs, and create profiles, with information about their sex, location, age and interests. They can also invite others to join them, virtually. The site is free to users. The site has become popular in terms of a true social network, with many users choosing to utilize the fun and entertaining aspects, such as the ability to post photos, leave messages, and add music.

Similar to MySpace, **Facebook** is a social networking Web site that also allows individuals to create their own profiles and upload photos. It also affords users the opportunity to locate other friends, colleagues, and acquaintances through its comprehensive search engine. While Facebook might have begun as a means for social networking among college students, it grew in popularity and is presently used by many professionals and businesses throughout the world. On Facebook, you can personally invite others to join your friends list and follow their profile.

LinkedIn, another networking site, boasts of having some 50 million members. Users can create their own profile on the site, and you can invite others to join you, or you can connect with other professionals in your field. LinkedIn has become popular in the business and professional world, with users inviting colleagues and acquaintances to join them. Having more and more people linking to your site is like filling your Rolodex full of great business contacts whose profiles you will have access to as well.

Twitter puts a different spin on social networking. The real-time messaging project allows users to post their thoughts, observations, and opinions in short messages. Built with the idea of allowing friends and colleagues to stay connected with each other, the social networking site serves more as a message board than a place to create a profile. By "tweeting," users post messages, or **tweets**, to express their thoughts in up to 140 characters, which generally translates to about 40 words, or the length of a short text message. Twitter users **follow** each other virtually, meaning they can literally read what is going on in people's minds, or what is newsworthy to them, simply by the tweets they are posting.

CASE STUDY: HOW SOCIAL NETWORKS CAN HELP JOB SEEKERS

Aaron Baer
Public relations and
marketing specialist
www.ZooLoo.com

While some people can be intimidated by social networking, **www.ZooLoo.com** Public Relations and Marketing Specialist Aaron Baer dives into the unique online platform that can be used to give job seekers a competitive edge.

"It allows you to communicate with professionals in your industry in a way never before possible," Baer said. "The best thing anyone can do to develop their presence is to start networking online. There are millions of conversations going on, and getting involved is a great first step."

With the ability to unveil any type of information — both personal and professional — job seekers often see social networking as a way for employers to dig up dirt on them. Baer, however, thinks the Internet stands for more: It provides job seekers with an opportunity to build relationships with employers in ways that a résumé and cover letter never could.

Once Internet users have made an initial connection with employers via sites like Facebook, Twitter, LinkedIn, and other social networking sites or blogs, they can demonstrate their passion in the related field, while, at the same time, establishing personality and building rapport.

"Considering how expensive it is for companies to train employees, making sure someone is a good fit in the office is invaluable," Baer said. "Showing other interests and letting employers get to know you can provide them with a different perspective."

With ZooLoo, job seekers can do that, Baer said. The Personal Web Dashboard began as a means to allow users to visit a single site that accommodated a variety of needs, including résumé posting and social networking. The Web site allows anyone to post their résumés, portfolios, and more online, using their own domain name, for free. There are no html codes involved, so users can drag and drop content, simplifying the process of building a Web site for those who are not tech-savvy, he said.

"In minutes, someone can create his or her online identity for employers to see," he said.

He further pointed out that the site is a complete online environment that brings almost everything you would want to do on the Web into one place: social networking, and the ability to create your own Web site with your own domain name and set custom privacy permissions — something Baer recommends job seekers to do in addition to consistent social networking.

Having a Web site completes your online presence, as it shows a level of professionalism and organization. Nobody carries their résumé around with them, and often times, you may be caught without business cards. With your own domain name, when you meet or network with an employer, all they need is a domain name to find you, and your résumé, online.

Regardless of which sites you use to brand yourself online, Baer said the most important thing is for job seekers to be consistent.

"Post regular content; let the readers you have know that they can always come to your blog to find new content," Baer said.

Sample social networking profile

The following profile is an example of what your completed online profile may look like. Different social networking sites have different fields of information, so if you have more than one profile, they may differ slightly.

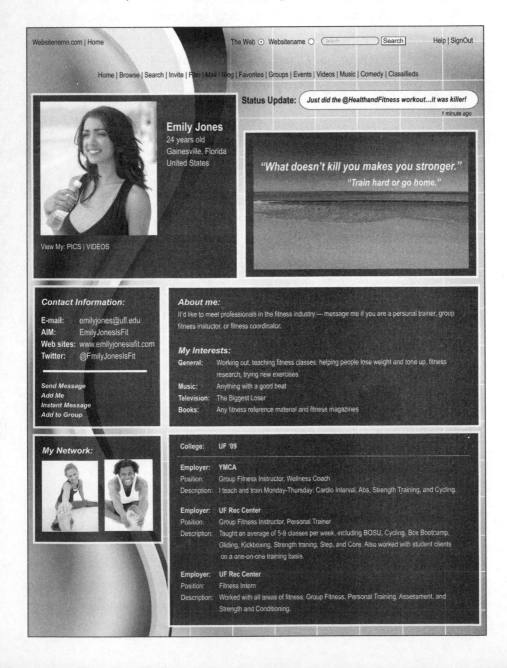

Pictures

Pictures usually can spice up a site and offer a glimpse into a person's life. On some sites, pictures of friends and gatherings are in order, particularly if the site is to be used for personal reasons. If you are planning on using the site professionally, you may want to consider having a professional picture taken of yourself, or at least making sure you have a photo in which you are wearing professional attire. You can also take this opportunity to display any work or accomplishments you have made. Nothing says more than a real picture of some product or even an achievement award, with a fitting caption underneath.

What You Write

What you write will also say a lot about you. If you are moving in the professional direction, then make sure everything on your site echoes "I am a professional." Try to avoid slang words, topics that are better left on the editorial pages, and tidbits about yourself that you really would never tell an employer face-to-face. Again, a nicely done, polished, professional profile is what most companies want to see. Some sites have tutorials you can take to provide you with the best tools for developing your profile.

Sometimes, it is nice to speak about a subject that you are just dying to talk about, or to be able to share a thought that you are just bursting at the seams about. The beauty of social networking is that you can do just that, from anywhere, at any time, and to anyone who happens to be following the dialogue of that subject via the Internet. Twitter, for example, allows users a tremendous amount of freedom of expression. You can **tweet** your way into just about every subject, but when job shopping, it may be wise to stay away from expressing your views on certain subjects. For example, if you are a very opinionated Democrat or Republican, it is fine to tweet about politics and let the whole know about your political views, but consider what your potential employer or recruiter might think if you have invited him or her to **follow** you. While it is fine to express your views, be aware that your potential employer — someone whom you are trying to win over — may have a completely opposite point of view. Will it cost you a job offer? You will never know, because those are the types of issues you can never pinpoint, nor will any potential employer ever say that your political tweets were the reason you were not hired. You just may never receive a call back for one reason or another.

On the opposite side of the coin, you can also use sites like Twitter to gain an advantage over your job-seeking competitors. You can provide daily tips on a particular subject related to the industry you are trying to break into, or analysis in regard to a particular event, topic or issue. You can use these tweets to show a potential employer that your advice is available to literally millions who use Twitter. It is also a means to show, rather than tell, your knowledge on a particular subject or item.

You can also use Facebook and MySpace as a means to express yourself professionally. If you are in some of the more creative work fields, you can use either venue to create an eye-catching and professional presentation.

If you are going into the social networking world half-heartedly, or without spending the time to do it right, you may want to skip the presence altogether. It is the equivalent of watching a million-dollar commercial on TV, followed by an amateurish $200 spot that was slapped together. While you do not have to take a course or be an expert in creating your social networking profile, you should plan out your page and choose your content carefully. It will go a long way in showing an employer what you are capable of.

Other uses of social networking

In addition to branding yourself as the ideal candidate for a particular position or as an expert in a certain field, you can use social networking sites and blogs to make contacts. Remember, these sites are called social networking sites for a reason: They facilitate communication.

Use your online profiles to your advantage, and spark up conversations with industry experts or employees at the companies you are applying for. While you want to prove that you are knowledgeable in your field, you may also want to try and make a more personal connection with these people, too. By building relationships and finding things you have in common, you may increase your chances of getting hired, or at least of learning more about an industry or company.

Social networking sites can also be used as a sounding board to find answers to questions you may have about a company. Usually, when you have developed relationships with people, even if you have never actually met them, they are willing to help you or offer assistance in any way they can. Take advantage of this, and use your networking skills to find more out about your company, whether it is the inside scoop, or just knowing what it is like to work there.

You may want to keep your inquiries more general, and use a screen name to disguise your identity. You could reach out to potential employers through various social networking avenues. Just do not divulge too much information about yourself. You may find employees who have worked at the company or are presently employed by the company you are interviewing with. You can simply post a question on a particular network. You will want to do this as a means of receiving advice from a past or present company employee. You may be able to secure knowledge that you would otherwise not be privy to without a personal connection.

There are a lot of people you may meet through the Internet who are more than willing to help you. The problem is that you really have no way of knowing exactly who you are talking to. It is nice to get unfiltered or uncensored information, but you may not get the whole story. Without knowing it, you may be taking advice from a disgruntled employee. Thus, remember to take everything with a grain of salt.

Building Your Own Web site — Your Central Hub

Creating your own Web site is a great way to enhance you presence on the Internet, while dazzling a potential employer at the same time. Your Web site should serve as a central place to connect all of your social media endeavors, as well as to store things you want your potential employers to see; it is the place that encompasses all of the elements of your online presence.

You can make your Web site as flashy or conservative as you like — just remember to aim for a professional look. There are several main steps that go into developing a Web site, and they can be done regardless of how technologically savvy you are. Your main steps are:

1. Selecting a domain name.
2. Deciding on what you want the theme to be and what to include in terms of content.
3. Actually creating and designing the site.
4. Choosing a location to display your Web site — or finding a host location on the Internet.
5. Letting people know your Web site exists.

Domain name

A domain name is the registered site name where your Web site can be physically located on the Internet. It is the Web address your site will have.

Because the purpose of the site will be to impress employers and show how professional you are, you may want to choose a domain name that includes your own name. It is simple and to the point. Taking a name that is not relevant, or a name that is not easy to type in or find, will defeat the purpose.

Content

What you choose to put on your Web site will depend on you and your career goals and objectives. If you are searching for a job that requires special skills and talents, why not showcase them on your site?

You may want to include some sort of biography or summary of yourself. Because you have the final say in what content appears on the Web site, you can create your own online persona. If you are an expert in a particular field, say that. If you have any accompanying materials, then make sure to include them as well.

You can add items such as testimonials from previous clients and customers, or even from other experts in your particular field. You want your site to reflect who you are and what you have to offer. While a potential employer may call for references, the Web site will give them an opportunity to see for themselves what you are truly capable of, and what other people are saying about you and your work.

You will also want to break up the text by adding photographs, videos, charts, or any other type of artwork or multimedia element that would help convey your message as a professional. You want the site to be as attractive, professional, and polished as possible, so keep this in mind while you select what elements you are going to showcase on your Web page. Do not clutter it with irrelevant materials or too many visuals.

Another important part of your content should be contact information. You will want to provide your e-mail address, along with links to your Twitter, Facebook, LinkedIn, blog, or other Internet accounts that you have used to develop your online presence. You may also choose to upload your résumé. As with creating profiles on other Internet platforms, remember that you will not be able to control who actually does visit your site, so you may want to stay away from providing too much personal information.

Once you have decided on the materials you will include in your Web site, you can choose how to design and create it, and where to place it on the Internet. You may want to make a stop at **www.ZooLoo.com**, which provides guidance and a free Web site-builder tool to help you create a visually appealing site. Another Internet location you may want to visit is TheFreeSite.com (**www.thefreesite.com**), which provides visitors with information regarding potential hosts for building a Web site.

Design and construction

Building a Web site may sound intimidating to the Internet and computer novice. But, in actuality, it is not, especially if you know where to go for help. Because you have already decided on what you will be posting on your Web site, now it is a matter of style and putting all the pieces together. Some Web sites, such as Zooloo.com, provide templates to help you build and design your site, as well as other ready-made designs and themes. These host sites also offer tutorials to guide you during the construction process.

No matter what you decide to place on your Web site, just remember that you are shooting for professionalism. The look, the content, and the site itself should convey a message to a potential employer that you are a professional in everything you do, including your site.

Your Web site does not have to be many pages — just enough to convey to an employer that you are the right person for the job you are applying for.

Hosts

The host is where your Web pages will be stored and can be found on the Internet. It will be the location where people such as hiring managers can find you. Therefore, you may want to decide on your host site at the very beginning of your Web-building process, after you have compiled the materials for your content. Because a number of host sites also include Web site development tools, it may be easier for you to take advantage of them from the start. Try visiting host sites such as Bluehost (**www.bluehost. com**) that offer a drag-and-drop site builder and free domain name.

Promotion

Once your site is complete, you will want to promote it with any and all potential employers. You may want to include your Web site address on your résumé, business cards, and even in correspondence with a potential employer. This way, what you were unable to convey to a hiring manager in the brief length of a cover letter or an interview, you will be able to show via your Web site .

Your Web site can be the focal point of your Internet presence. You can either include your work on the site, or add links to allow viewers to visit other areas on the Internet where you have made your mark. If your professional profile is on LinkedIn, why not add the hyperlink to allow visitors to find your profile? If you have a blog, or you are active on Twitter, these are other areas where you will want to include links on your Web site. Again, make sure that visitors, particularly potential employers, will be able to find you easily by adding your e-mail address or a link to contact you in a visible spot.

CHAPTER 9

Reduce Cyber Crime by Preventing
Strangers From Entering Your Virtual Life

Internet Lingo

Anti-spam: A software program that allows you to prevent unwanted solicitations, such as e-mail advertisements, from ever making it into your inbox. You can download or purchase such a program, and the unwanted e-mail, or most of it, will be directly routed into your junk or trash folder.

Anti-virus: A software program that can be used to block harmful problems in your computer. The software can be set to scan your computer and seek out such harmful viruses and block or disable them. It can also be used to remove such viruses that may have found their way into your computer.

Blind ads: Job listings and advertisements that do not mention the specific company who is doing the hiring. Often times, the advertisement will be labeled "confidential" instead of naming a company or contact person.

Firewall: A computer system function that blocks or prevents unwanted intrusions into your computer. It allows you to perform legitimate functions while preventing adverse entries into your computer.

Privacy policy: The rules governing a Web site's use of information, which may be collected from someone who uses or registers on their site.

Security settings: Various measures you can take to increase the security level on your computer. Your security settings can usually be found at the top of your home page, under the Tools section.

Temporary files, cookies: Files that save or store information about sites you visit during your time browsing the Internet.

Trojan horses: A program or other type of item, such as a virus, that can cause problems for your computer. The program or item is usually buried in something else so that when it reaches a computer, it can cause problems without being easily detected.

URL: A Uniform Resource Locator, which in essence is the location of a Web site. Just like a company has a physical address, the business will also have a URL Web address assigned to it as well.

Unlike years ago, where you could install a security system and deadbolt your doors to prevent a thief from sneaking into your home and stealing your assets, the Internet leaves users vulnerable to all kinds of attacks. While you may never open your door to a stranger who may try to steal your credit cards, or other items of value, the thieves are still out there. But, instead of showing up on your doorstep, they are working through cyberspace. Without taking proper precautions, you may be inviting those types of criminals into your home and your life through the Internet.

Not everyone who uses the Internet is victimized, but you should be aware that it happens so you can take action to protect yourself from becoming a new statistic for cyberspace crime. Some of the most basic steps will include having a **firewall** on your computer to prevent unwanted traffic from getting through. A firewall is a type of application that works through your computer to prevent others from accessing your machine or the information contained on your computer. These are often automatically turned on through your computer's operating system. Although firewalls are the first line of defense from such thieves, you can provide another layer of protection with a good **anti-spam** and **anti-virus** program as well. Both these types of software programs work to prevent unwanted solicitations and unwanted programs that can damage your computer from entering your machine and virtual world. There are many out there — some are free, while others operate on donations or fees. If there is a fee, it is money well-spent if it lessens your chances of becoming a victim of Internet crime.

Applying to Confidential Ads

Sometimes legitimate companies will post **blind**, or confidential, job advertisements. You will be able to see the position, the duties and responsibilities, the city, and the state the job is located in, but not the company. Under employer, it may say confidential. These ads are usually posted on the major sites, and they do not include contact information, contact personnel, phone numbers, or addresses. There are a number of reasons why a company will do this. In many cases, it is because the company is planning on getting rid of a particular employee, and they do not want the individual to have advance notice about the situation. The good news for a job seeker is that the employer is usually looking to fill the position quickly. The adverse news is that the employee you will be replacing may not know he or she is on the way out. Thus, the ad is blind because the company does not want to leak any information about an employee that will soon be let go.

There are other reasons why a company would post such a confidential ad, and not all of them involve employees who will be leaving. Sometimes a company just wants to keep a low profile during the hiring process.

But beware that on the other hand, there are other companies or individuals who are looking to use the job posting as a means to either sell you another product, secure your personal information (as it appears on a résumé), or set you up for a scam.

You should always weigh the pros and cons of applying to a confidential position because, in some instances, you will get unwanted responses. These responses could come in the form of e-mails from unknown addresses that say all of the employees of a "confidential company" at which you just applied for a job is requiring all employees to have their credit reports pulled. The e-mail may direct you to a link that, for a price, will allow you to have the most up-to-date information about your credit sent to you. In this scenario, if you click on the link and pay the fee to have your credit report pulled, you have just fallen victim to a company's latest scam. If a company is going to hire you and conduct a background check (which may include both a criminal and credit check), the company will do all of the work at their own expense. You, as an employee, will not be expected to provide a credit report.

 Job Tip!

Never put your social security number on your résumé. As mentioned, there are unscrupulous people that spend days thinking of ways to procure that type of information from unsuspecting individuals. Do not make it easy for them.

Protecting Yourself

Even before you begin your daily browsing for job listings, you may want to take a few steps on your computer to ensure that you are being as cautious as possible. You can start by making sure your computer **security settings** are on high. This will help you avoid as many unsolicited e-mail and traffic as possible. You can try the steps below to increase your virtual protection.

Security steps

You can begin by changing your own settings or making sure that the settings you currently have are protecting you from potential attacks.

- Start by clicking on "Tools" at the top of the screen.
- Click on "Internet Options."
- From there, you should see various tabs.
- Click on the "Security" tab or picture.
- Make sure that check marks are made next to items that will warn you if the site you are visiting appears to be a forgery, or if a site you are visiting attempts to download items into your computer or alter your settings.

When you are finished working on your material for the day, go into the Tools settings on your computer, usually found at the top of your screen, when you are on the Internet. From there, eliminate or clear all **temporary files**, **cookies**, and other private data. Sometimes these cookies are also used to track information about Web site visitors. While most cookies are good in the sense that they store information on individual preferences relative to their site, there are other cookies that will also track your movements and visits to completely different sites, other than their own. They can collect your actions and movements on other sites. This is similar to having someone follow you into every store you visit and watch every purchase you make.

Of course, you are not going to be followed into every store at the mall. Most cookies you acquire through your site visits will be good cookies — not the ones that follow your Internet tracks.

There are good and bad aspects to almost every site. Knowing what to look for is the best way to know what is in store for you, especially if sites offer unique features. Sometimes there may be problems when you visit a reputable Web site and apply for a job from a confidential or unknown company. Companies who are pushing products, such as credit reports or job membership sites for a fee, will try to tie their product to your job application.

You may visit a reputable job site, like Yahoo! HotJobs, apply for a position that may be from a confidential or unknown company, and suddenly receive an e-mail indicating your application was received. It will further indicate that you can continue with the application process by visiting another site. However, a scam recently seen will take it further. Once you click your way to the other site, a screen will appear asking you if you want to receive your monthly credit report for a monthly fee of $19.99.

Susan Koeppen, consumer correspondent for *The Early Show* on CBS, did a report on such scams in September 2009. Koeppen focused on companies who were charging job seekers to help the candidates find federal government positions. While the ads sounded great, they were too good to be true. In the case of the individual Koeppen's report highlighted, the unsuspecting job seeker provided his bank information and paid a fee of over $120 to try to get closer to a federal job. He received nothing in return for his investment.

As stated before **www.USAJobs.gov** is the best bet for procuring a job in the public sector of federal government. Protecting your personal information is important. If a company is trying to force you to purchase any type of membership or product in order to help you find a job, do research on the company. Check with your state's consumer affairs division to find out if the company already has adverse filings. Unfortunately, there are also legitimate companies out there who will suffer as a result of the scams, and there are times when you may need to get some information about yourself out there in order to make a connection.

But what if you are not applying for a government job — how do you protect yourself when you are posting your résumé to the public? You can also decide with some sites how public you want your résumé to be. For instance, with Monster.com, you can have several types of résumés in your personal file. You can also decide whether you want your résumé to be public, where employers can view every aspect of your résumé, or you can decide to keep it confidential, where employers can see most of your résumé data, except for your contact information or current employer information. The site also allows you to keep your résumé on private status, where employers cannot view your résumé at all. It will only be made available for employers at jobs you apply for. That way, if it is someone other than a potential employer is figuratively crawling the Internet for data such as phone numbers or e-mails addresses, your information will not fall into their hands.

Most job sites will also ask whether you want to start receiving additional e-mails from the site in a small box along the bottom of the screen. You may or may not choose to. A lot of times the box is pre-filled to "yes." Before you know it, you could be receiving numerous unwanted or unnecessary e-mails on a daily basis. It really forces you to pay attention and read everything on the screen when it comes to searching for jobs. Another common question will be whether you want to further your education. A lot of times the "yes" box is pre-filled for this, too. Again, if you do not opt out or click "no thanks," you could find yourself receiving unnecessary e-mails and letters through regular mail, regarding your new educational opportunities.

There is nothing like waking up to all kinds of junk mail in your e-mail inbox. You will spend the rest of the morning getting rid of junk, which is no longer cluttering up your outside mailbox, but is now entering your home electronically. Your own e-mail address may be sold or handed over to multiple companies and parties, just as physical addresses were sold to list buyers in the past. Again, choose your sites wisely and read the fine print, unless you want to sort through such junk mail on a daily basis.

Getting spammed

While not becoming a victim of cyberspace crime is a priority for virtually all Internet users, there is another type of behavior that is almost as loathsome. It is called spam or getting "spammed." Spamming, in its most basic form, is sending unwanted or unsolicited e-mails to individuals. There are other types of spamming via the Internet, but the most common instance for the job seeker is the e-mail spam. Other types of abuse may come in the form of text messaging over the phone, search engine sites that redirect you to a product or service you did not ask for, or through communication on some of the social network sites. If you are not careful, you can find yourself the recipient of a lot of daily junk mail. While some may be harmless nuisances, other types of e-mails may carry **Trojan horses** and viruses designed to do malicious damages to your computer. In some cases, the problem could result in allowing a stranger to access your computer and its contents from a remote location, or to manipulate and track your every move on the computer, or even to cause your system to be completely controlled by a virus.

If you provide your banking information, you may be setting yourself up to receive phony e-mails made to look exactly like the ones you receive from your bank. While the real bank e-mails will come from an address you know, such as info@ZYbank.com, the phony e-mails are made to look as close to the real thing as possible. Their e-mail address may be from service@info.ZYbank.com. If, by chance, you receive these types of e-mails, report them to your bank immediately.

How does this happen?

How many times in the past have you or your family sat down to dinner only to be interrupted by a ringing phone? You get up to answer and find a telemarketer at the other end of the call, trying to sell you some product of service you do not want or need.

In order to stop such unwanted solicitation, in 1991 Congress signed the Telephone Consumer Protection Act, which regulated such calls from telemarketers. From there, a national Do-Not-Call list was created for individuals who did not want to receive such calls. With this law, individuals could request that their names and phone numbers be taken off lists used by tele-marketers. If the telemarketers persisted, they could face stiff penalties.

While the government has addressed such phone calls from unwanted so-licitors, there is still not enough action on the part of such spamming via the Internet. It can occur from a simple job application where you fill out your name and e-mail address. Your information, as well as information from other job seekers, is compiled into a list and then sold to advertisers or third-party companies. Sometimes the company itself, as well as the product, is bogus. While you read the ad and placed your order, a thief got your credit card and personal information, such as your name, mailing address, age, date of birth, credit card account number, and the expiration date on your card.

Sometimes companies will sell the information, such as the list of e-mail addresses from individuals who may have visited their site and registered or applied for a job. While most companies and Web sites have a policy of not sharing information, there are others who will. You can find out if a com-pany or Web site will share your information by clicking on their "privacy policy," usually located at the bottom of the page.

If you are not careful, your information could be sold or shared with a com-pletely separate company that uses the Internet to advertise their products and services. These companies will purchase the lists of e-mail addresses and names and send you unwanted e-mails.

Also, these companies often use the spamming method to advertise their products because the cost of sending out e-mails is free. The company is not paying for the cost of even a stamp — it is just a matter of acquir-ing a list of e-mail addresses and clicking "send" on a computer. Often times, the e-mails may come from different countries, as well as from the United States.

Another major problem is that e-mails are very hard to trace back to the particular individual or company who sent bulk, junk e-mail in the first place. Because a number of sites, such as Google and Yahoo!, offer free e-mail addresses, there are those who will take advantage of the opportunity to set up numerous accounts for the purpose of cluttering up someone else's inbox.

In some instances, spammers will join online groups in order to be able to access the e-mail addresses of members. Once they are in the group, they will use the opportunity to promote a product they have been hired to pitch.

How to prevent it

There are ways to reduce your chances of becoming a victim of spamming.

- Be conscientious about whom you share your personal information with, including your e-mail address.

- Set your online profile headings to private or confidential, where only employers at companies you have applied to will be able to access your contact information.

- Exercise extreme caution when providing or submitting your e-mail address.

- Take caution when responding to a confidential or blind ad. You may risk ending up on an e-mail spam list. If you do not want to take the risk, stay away from those types of job postings.

- Do not open unsolicited e-mails or e-mails from unknown entities.

- If you do happen to open such an e-mail, do not click on any links.

Unwelcome advertisements that follow a job application

Once you have applied for a job, you may start receiving those unwanted advertisements. You may also receive e-mails stating that your résumé and application were received, but that ask you to visit another site for more information about the job posting. Once you get to the site you are referred to, you may find there is no information about the job offer, but instead, you find an offer to join a job club or become a member of the site. The catch is that there is a price for these memberships, even though they promise additional job listings will come your way if you join. Again, this is nothing more than businesses using your e-mail and personal contact information to make a profit. Many times, there are no jobs or job listings that you will have access to by joining these sites or becoming a member. The job postings that some of these companies offer can be found by anyone using the Internet. This is about the business profiting from you, though it should also be noted that there are some legitimate companies who also charge a fee to access some of their job listings.

If you were to apply for a job in person and the company representative you submitted your application to tried to sell you something, instead of interview you for the job, then you would probably stomp out of the establishment, giving them a piece of your mind about deceptive practices. Yet the chances of this scenario occurring when you apply for jobs online are even higher than applying in person. It can be extremely difficult to make unknown Internet companies accountable and credible, because many times, there may not even be a real physical office location. And getting solicited for a dating service or a product may not be against the law, despite of the nuisance it presents. Hence, exercise caution when applying to jobs online.

Be wary of any unsolicited e-mails you receive. Do not respond. If there are attachments, do not open them — simply delete them. Another trick of spammers is to determine whether an e-mail address they have is a functioning or legitimate address. They may indicate in an e-mail that if you want to stop receiving such advertisements, you can go to another site to get your name off the list. The problem is, once you click or respond to the original e-mail, they know your e-mail address is active.

If, by chance, you find yourself on a list, one approach you may want to take is blocking the sender. While this function will work on some junk e-mail, it may not for others because spammers change their addresses often, sometimes daily, to cover their tracks. Because of this circumstance, it may be difficult to prevent it altogether. To get off a company list, many legitimate companies will also instruct you to take the same steps as the bogus companies — you will have to click onto their site and request that your name be removed. The difference is, however, that legitimate companies will actually take your e-mail address off their list.

You can also go into your e-mail system and block the sender. While you will not be able to physically prevent the e-mail from being sent to your computer, by blocking a sender, any items from that particular e-mail address will go directly into your deleted or trash files, rather than your inbox. On Gmail, you can do this by altering your "Settings," found at the top right corner of your window. After clicking on the "Settings" tab, click on "Filters," and you can choose specific criteria for determining what to do with a message as it arrives. You can also use this to conduct tests to make sure you set your filters correctly.

To block an e-mail sender on general accounts:

1) Open the e-mail (but do not click on any of the links or attachments).

2) Move your mouse over to the sender's name (located next to "From") at the top of the e-mail.

3) Right click on your mouse.

4) Click "block sender."

5) From here on, e-mails sent from that person's specific e-mail address will be sent to your trash file, rather than to your inbox.

How to Tell if the Job Ad is a Scam

You have seen them everywhere: jobs that sound too good to be true, or advertisements sprinkled with misspelled words, vague, or incorrect information. There are promises of making hundreds of dollars a day working in a part time position. Remember, if it sounds too good to be true, chances are it is some type of scam. Many of the following characteristics will serve as red flags that the job in the advertisement is a scam.

Spelling

There are obvious as well as subtle ways to determine whether a job ad is real or a scam. While it is true that once in a while, a legitimate company may make a spelling mistake in their job advertisement or their follow-up e-mail, misspelled words and grammatically incorrect sentences are more like a sign of a scam because thieves, who are in a hurry to post numerous phony ads, often overlook such little details.

Research

Again, your company research comes into play. Does the company that posted the ad have any kind of online presence — is there an official company Web site? If so, type in the name of the company and see if you can locate their Web site. Many large companies have Web site addresses, or Uniform Resource Locators (URLs). Also, you may want to visit sites like the Better Business Bureau to find additional information.

Location

If a company wants to hire you for a job, there should be a physical location where you will be working, unless you are telecommuting. You should be able to use MapQuest (**www.mapquest.com**) or Google Maps to find a specific office location for the company. Double-check the information, particularly if you are unfamiliar with the organization. If you get a physical address, look up the company in the White Pages to verify that the address listed online is the same, and if the company's phone number is for a legitimate landline, and not a cell phone.

E-mail address

If you have applied to a company and you receive an e-mail back from them, see what e-mail address they used. Many legitimate companies with Web sites will also have very similar e-mail addresses. For instance, if you applied to the All Business Cause company for a position, you can expect the domain of the e-mail address to read something like @allbusinesscause. com or @abc.com. On the other hand, if you apply to the same company and you receive an e-mail back from senders such as ginak12799@hotmail. com or jsdhdjk18273@gmail.com, there is a good chance that the company you applied to is not legitimate.

Things to do (or not do) to prevent scams

Exercising common sense and being Internet-savvy are the easiest ways you can protect yourself from being scammed. Ask yourself:

- Is the job posting is too good to be true?

- Does it promise you vast wealth for very little work or for unskilled labor?
- Does the posting have glaring errors?
- Does the company seem nonexistent?
- Is the e-mail address fake, or does it use an odd format?

Because of the ease in which the Internet allows for informational sharing, it is easy to fall victim to such scams if you do not take the time to answer these questions. Use the following tips, in addition to the questions above, to avoid giving scammers access to your information.

Read the fine print

It cannot be emphasized enough how important it is to read the fine print on any Web site you are visiting or applying to jobs through. Look for any pre-populated fields with check marks. You should look for sentences that have boxes or check marks at the end of them. The Web site pre-answers the question for the visitor in the affirmative. Web sites may be signing you up to participate in free trial offers, which will share your information with others, or use your information without your approval. The responsibility will rest with you in many instances. While it may be tedious to go through the small print regarding privacy and user policies, it is better than having to weed out the numerous pieces of spam e-mails that will arrive daily.

Use caution when including your contact information

Contact information, of course, is important when you stop to consider the fact that it is the only way a potential employer will know where and how to find you. But it is a dual-edged sword because you are leaving yourself open to unsolicited e-mails and phone calls if you are not familiar with the company, and it is using a job posting as a means to acquire your phone and e-mail address information. Until recently, most cell phone numbers have been off limits to such solicitors, mainly because cell phone holders were charged for both incoming and outgoing phone calls. The rules have changed, however, and even cell phone numbers are being sought after and procured for the same purposes as e-mails from spammers.

Thus, it is important to use caution when providing such information. Think about who will be receiving the data — you may not want to have your cell phone included in your résumé or your online profiles, particularly if you are on a plan where you will be charged for all incoming calls, including the unsolicited ones.

Never include personal details such as your social security number, bank account, credit account numbers, or anything else that could leave you victimized. Even if a particular Web site asks for this information, chances are that the site and job are phonies. Legitimate businesses who are looking for job candidates will never ask for such things as bank account or credit card information. You may, however, be asked to provide your social security number to legitimate companies. The company may want to run a background check on you if they are interested in hiring you. If this is company policy, it is usually listed under the terms and conditions of the application, and you usually have to agree to things like background checks and drug testing before submitting the application.

In most cases, however, your name, phone number, physical address, and e-mail address should suffice because you have given potential employers three different ways to contact you. Do not provide more than that.

To determine if a company Web site is legitimate, check the actual site address at the top of your Web browser window. Determine if it is an "http" or an "https" address. The single "s" indicates the site is a secure one; "http" is not. Keep in mind that a company Web site can be real even though it is not secure. Also, if it is an https site, you can usually click on it and find out who owns the site so that you know who you are handing your information over to. Make sure you are on the site you want to be on — not a cheap imitation of it.

Over-sending your résumé

The prospect of sending your résumé to hundreds and thousands of possible employers may sound extremely alluring, and for some people it works out just fine; a match may be made in no time at all. But keep in mind that if you do this, you are tossing out your résumé randomly, throwing caution to the winds. You may be leaving yourself open to identity theft because of the sheer number of locations your résumé and personal information can now be found on the Internet.

There are certain people who are paid to surf the Internet and to share such information. They may not want to steal your personal information, but rather to sell you products and services, and to send unsolicited advertisements through your e-mail address.

What Can Happen if You Are Not Careful

Again, if you choose to throw caution to the wind and blast your information everywhere, you may be handing over the keys of your personal life to any stranger in cyberspace. You certainly would not go to sleep at night with your doors completely unlocked. You would take steps to protect yourself and your belongings, which is why you need to take similar precautions when using the Internet. That way, you will not be leaving yourself vulnerable by not protecting your personal information.

Once you have become a victim, you may end up paying for the consequences for years to come. If someone is able to take the information you have provided via the Internet and opens credit cards in your name, you may be faced with financial ruin for years, or having to explain to credit card companies, banks, and even potential employers how a personal identity theft incident led to the demise of your credit. And if thieves have found out enough information to access your bank accounts, you will be faced with trying to fight the bank to get your money back. People have lost thousands of dollars this way.

CHAPTER 10

Getting Hired —
Moving Closer to Success

Internet Lingo

Follow-up e-mail: The e-mail a job seeker sends after submitting a job application or after having an interview. This e-mail is sent to either a staffing agency or the company.

Industry trends: Ways companies may change the methods in which they conduct their business, deliver their products and/or services, or operate their organizations. It is often a new practice or way of doing business, driven by many factors, including profits, the economy, or customer demands.

Job progress log: A paper or online document used to track which jobs you have applied for, specifics about the jobs, and the outcome of your job applications.

Now that you have dazzled them with your Internet skills, it is time to impress potential employers with your keen business etiquette, savvy knowledge, and style. From the time you turned on your computer and took the necessary steps to make yourself a formidable Internet presence to be reckoned with — not to mention valuable stock for any company — you have shown that you are willing to go the distance.

As you have already learned, virtual life is like driving on a fast-paced highway without any speed limits. Even at such lightning speed, there is still protocol that needs to be followed. Needless to say, you will be putting your best foot forward as you proceed to the next level — a level that takes you out of your virtual comfort zone.

Following Up

Many times, when you apply through the Internet, it is a very impersonal experience without a particular person's name attached to the posting. In that case, you can call the company to find out which recruiter or human resources representative is handling the position. You will want to find out the person's name, their title, and their e-mail address. Without such personalization, the recruiter or hiring representative will see you as nothing more than one in a stack of applications. With a little personalization, they may view you more as a living, breathing, viable candidate — a real person.

If you have just applied for a position, you may want to wait until the next day to send a more personalized e-mail. You will be sending a follow-up e-mail, but you may not want to make it immediate in case your potential employers are meeting with additional candidates in the next 24 hours — your **follow-up e-mail** may get lost in the shuffle. Or, employers may not remember your note at all if they are meeting with several candidates during the next 24 or 48 hours.

How long to wait

When and what you hear back from a job application may differ, depending on the type of job you are applying for, who the position is with, and how critically the employer needs to fill the job. Deciding how long to wait before you follow up is also somewhat different than when you physically visited an office and submitted your application in person. When you have submitted a **job application** at a particular company, you will have face-to-face contact with someone, whether it is a receptionist or a recruiter, and you will be given the opportunity to ask when the company is expecting to fill to position.

But through the Internet, there is no one to ask. You apply for the job, and away your application and résumé goes, so you often have no idea of when you should expect to hear back from the company — which is why the follow-up e-mail is so important.

You may want to wait for a few days before contacting the company you applied to, using the Internet. That way, the hiring manager will have had a little time to review the applications of would-be job candidates.

Be persistent, not annoying

If, by chance, you send out your original e-mail and find that it goes unanswered, you can take the opportunity to let them know that you are still interested in the position. In such an e-mail, you would restate why you feel you would be the best person for the position, as well as letting the employer know you are looking forward to meeting or speaking with him or her again.

Also, if you find any additional articles or industry news relevant to the company, feel free to e-mail them about the information. This would present the perfect opportunity to indicate to the potential employer that you are still interested in the job, and that you are looking out for his or her interests. It also shows that you are keeping abreast on **industry trends**. Just make sure to keep your message short and to the point, and that the article or link you are sending is truly pertinent to the company or industry.

Thank them for their time

Whether you are on your first e-mail with the company or your third regarding the same position, make sure to take the opportunity in each correspondence to thank your potential employers for their time and assistance. While you do not do things to be thanked or appreciated, it is always a little easier to go the extra distance — say, send an e-mail update about the position — to someone who is appreciative of your efforts. Proper manners and protocol are always in order when it comes to the Internet and business.

What to say, whom to send it to

Once you have decided the time is right for the follow up, you can use either of two methods to express your interest in the position. You will want to keep the e-mail brief, like the following sample e-mail:

Dear Mr. Jones:

I wanted to thank you for meeting with me this morning to discuss my candidacy for the (insert the job title) position I applied for. I was intrigued by the diverse and challenging scope of the job, and felt very confident that I could provide the necessary skills to contribute to your team's many successes.

I wanted to let you know that I am available if you would like to discuss the position further, or if you have any questions.

Sincerely,

Brad Smith

Tracking Your Job Search Progress

Keeping track of your job search may be much more important than you think. Say you applied online to various companies, including one that was confidential, for a file clerk position. In addition, you also sent out a couple of résumés and filled out applications for an executive secretary position. In total, you submitted 12 applications. You were familiar with all the companies, except for the one that was confidential, which was the blind advertisement that listed a good job but kept the company's name out of the listing.

Several days go by, and you begin to get a few responses. One company mentions the clerk position has been put on hold for now. A few of the others send you standard e-mails indicating that they chose other candidates. There is an acknowledgement from the confidential company that the position has been filled by another candidate. If you are keeping tabs and tracking your progress, you may notice that all of the executive secretary positions have been filled, while there are still a couple of companies who have not responded to you about the file clerk positions. After a week or two, you decide to delete all the e-mails you sent out for the file clerk positions, since you still have not heard anything from a few companies. The very next day, however, you receive an e-mail from a Shirley Johnson from EDF Company, indicating her company is interested in your application.

While this is great news, the problem is that you do not remember what position you applied for at the EDF Company. Was it the executive secretary or the file clerk position? You cannot e-mail Ms. Johnson and ask her which position she was talking about, so you are faced with a bad situation of trying to feel her out about the position — or the ultimate humiliation of having to admit that you are not sure what job she is talking about. Either way, it sets you up in an unprofessional light.

If you were keeping track of your job progress, however, you would know that it was the senior file clerk position you had applied for with EDF. When you think about applying for a job, or even a handful of jobs, there is not much to keep track of. But, if you apply to a few dozen, or several dozen, keeping track of the application process can become complicated. As for the mechanics of keeping a log, you can try a virtual log, all done in your computer, or a paper log, if you feel more comfortable. Some additional items you may want to include in your job progress log include the salary, location, any pros or cons, where you found the advertisement, and how you applied.

Sample Job Progress Log

Company	Job	Date	Applied	Location	Salary	Follow up	Hiring rep	Outcome

The Interview

The Internet can be addicting, and the job search draining — a poor combination. While most of the work you do in your online job search will not involve a face-to-face meeting, you should consider what will happen when you do get the interview you have been waiting for. While you are in your comfort zone when applying for jobs, make sure you stay up-to-par when it comes time to step out of the zone. The interview is your jump from the virtual world to reality. If you are lucky enough to get your foot through the door, make sure you are putting your best foot forward.

If, by chance, your interview is through a staffing agency, also known as the middleman in your job hiring process, do not take the meeting lightly. Be professional in your appearance, as well as with your demeanor and your tools. While the agency may not be the final decision maker, the representative you meet with will be championing your cause for getting hired. The recruiter may want to help you find a job, but he or she will equally want to satisfy their client — the company you applied to. Your potential employer will want you to look as if you are dressing to impress.

If you are starting with a staffing agency, you may want to ask questions about the types of positions they have and what their opinion is regarding your tools or your test score results. They may provide you with a large range of advice to help increase your chances of getting called for a job.

You have already impressed your potential employers through your virtual tools and timely etiquette; now, it is time to dazzle them in person. Everything matters in your first face-to-face interview, from the way you are dressed to the way you handle yourself throughout the course of the meeting.

Dress appropriately

A cardinal rule about interviews is to dress appropriately. Unless you are applying for a job in a warehouse — where jeans may be acceptable — dress professionally. Show a potential employer that you are a positive presence and would make a nice addition to the staff, rather than a detriment. Sloppy dress, or even casual dress, will not win any points when it comes to a potential employer. Even if you have heard through the grapevine that the company has a casual standard, it is always better to show up in your professional best.

Whether it is an interview with a staffing agency or your potential employer, dress in business professional: Suits, skirts, and pants for women, and for men, a suit, dress shirt, and tie are considered professional dress.

Be on time

Time is very important when it comes to an interview. If you arrive too early, the interviewer may actually be annoyed with you because they may have other obligations before you arrived. If you are scheduled for an 8 a.m. appointment, arriving 15 minutes early shows that you are punctual, and that you are taking the interview seriously. Showing up hours early, on the other hand, may convey that you do not listen or follow direction. Or, your recruiter could feel as though you are trying to squeeze the interview into your schedule because an hour earlier is more convenient for you.

By the same token, if you arrive late, you are showing a recruiter or potential employer the shape of things to come. Showing up late implies you do not care about punctuality, or that you are irresponsible. Both of these things will imply you do not care about the job you are applying for, and neither scenario will win you any points. If by chance you do run late because of an unforeseen accident, or you get lost, do not make a bad situation worse. If possible, pull over to the side of the road and call the recruiter or employer to let them know you ran into traffic or got lost, and you will be there as soon as possible. That way, they are not waiting for you, or they will not assume you simply overslept or are not coming.

 Job Tip!

Get directions to the interview site online. You may also want to make a dry run before the interview when you are not pressed for time. This way, you can give yourself extra time in case you experience delays. Be sure to bring the phone number and name of the person you are meeting for the interview. In the event of a problem, you can call and let him or her know what is going on.

Be prepared to ask and answer questions

When the day arrives and you have your interview, be prepared to ask meaningful questions about the position, the company, and the future of the company. This will convey your interest to a potential employer, while letting him or her know that you will be committed to the company if you are hired. Act interested and take notes if you can, for future use. You may need to use them in your follow up e-mail or if you are brought in again for a second or third interview.

Question Dos and Don'ts

Question *Dos*
Do ask about whether there is room for advancement.
Do ask about the specific duties and responsibilities you will be performing.
Do ask about a specific project or program the company may be embarking on.
Do ask about when the employer expects to fill the position.

| Do ask whether there is any additional information you can provide to the hiring manager. |
| Do ask for a card or e-mail address so you can send a thank-you note after the interview. |

Question *Dont's*
Do not ask about a time-off policy for leisure or illness.
Do not ask about raises or promotions.
Do not ask how you did in the interview.
Do not tell them you will be in touch.
Do not ask them anything too personal, about the position or themselves.
Do not tell them you plan on being out of town.

If you learned about a big project the company has going on during your company research, do not be afraid to mention it. You may also want to inquire how the position you are applying for will fit in with the new project. By doing this, you will show the person you are interviewing with that you care about the same things he or she does when it comes to the company. If, for example, the company is developing a service you are familiar with and have had experience with, why not show up to the interview with a brief proposal? Give the potential employer a taste of things to come.

Try to keep the focus on what you can do for the company, supporting what you say with the things you accomplished with your prior work experience. Now is not the time to be modest — boast of your accomplishments. Make sure to show yourself off, and do not complain about your last job, no matter how unpleasant or unfair it may have been.

You may be asked to talk about yourself, as well as why you think you would be the perfect fit for the position. The potential employer will want to know what you bring to the table and how you will fit in with the rest of the workforce.

Interview questions employers ask may include:

- Why do you think you are the most qualified person for this position?
- What experience of skills do you have that would make you a good fit for this position?
- What are your long-term career plans?
- Do you already have a job?
- Why did you leave your last position?
- Would you be willing to work overtime?
- Are you flexible about hours and salary?
- What are your strengths?
- What are your weaknesses?
- What would your previous supervisor or colleagues say about your work?
- Are you willing to relocate?
- Where do you see yourself in the future?

Bring something to leave behind

Picture yourself in the shoes of an employer or hiring manager who, in addition to all of their other duties, may have to meet most of the people who are hired for a company. At the end of the day it is nice to be able to have something to remember a candidate by, like a business card or résumé. They will have time to digest the information at their own pace, after the interview process is over. By leaving them something of yourself, it will convey your professionalism toward the position as well as how you approach such instances.

Have paper copies of résumés on hand

While you may have already submitted your résumé online when you applied, it is a good idea to bring several hard copies with you to the interview. It may be wise when the recruiter is scheduling you for the interview to ask whether it will be with one person or if you will be meeting with several different individuals. This way, you will have enough copies of your résumé to pass around, and one to keep yourself in the event they want to talk about particulars in the document. You always want to be able to provide your résumé during the interview so you have something to leave behind with the potential employer.

Bring lists of references and work history

In advance, prepare a reference cheat sheet. Having all of your information you will be asked to fill out is always a time saver, and this cheat sheet allows you to prepare early on. You will need to focus on the specifics. Your cheat sheet should include the specific start and end dates for each job you held, as prefaced in your résumé. From there, you should also include the name, address, and phone number of each company, along with a specific person listed as your supervisor. If you have the e-mail address of the company or your supervisor, include that as well.

This way, all the information you will need has been boiled down to a single sheet of paper.

Job Contacts and References

Schools

Ronald Reagan High School	The University of Texas at San Antonio
19000 Ronald Reagan	One UTSA Circle
San Antonio, TX 78258	San Antonio, TX 78249
(XXX) XXX-XXXX	(XXX) XXX-XXXX

References:
Jim Smith, Company Owner
XYZ Company.
55 USA Way, Suite 200

Certifications
Cisco Certified Internetwork
(CCIE)   9/8/2004

Houston, TX 77005　　　　　　　Certified Computing Professional
(XXX) XXX-XXXX　　　　　　　　(CCP)　　　　　　6/12/2006

Penny Jones,　　　　　　　　　　Certified Lotus Professional
IT Department Chief　　　　　　(CLP)　　　　　　5/20/2007
USA Phone Company
(Houston Division)
10103 Main Street
Houston, TX 77005
(XXX) XXX-XXXX

Michelle Prince, IT Program Manager
USA Phone Company (Houston Division)
10103 Main Street
Houston, TX 77005
(XXX) XXX-XXXX

Mike Hall, IT Supervisor
Southwest Community Communications
100123 Willington Road
San Antonio, TX 78230
(XXX) XXX-XXXX

Job Addresses
 XYZ Company 8/2008 – Present
55 USA Way, Suite 200
Houston, TX   77005
(XXX) XXX-XXXX

USA Phone Company, 1/2004 -7/2008
10103 Main Street
Houston, TX 77005
(XXX) XXX-XXXX

Southwest Community Comm., 6/2001 – 12/2003
100123 Willington Road
San Antonio, TX 78230
(XXX) XXX-XXXX

Business cards

Depending on the type of position you are applying for, you may want to consider leaving a business card with the hiring representative. The cards are a way of showing a potential employer how professional you are, especially when it comes to your job search and your own candidacy. There are Internet sites that offer free templates you can use to create your own cards for a low cost, and they will help you to create them. Some sites offer free promotions that allow you to get the cards for free.

Some sites for business cards include **www.vistaprint.com**, **www.free-printablebusinesscards.net**, and **www.free-business-card-templates. com**. The card can be as simple or as fancy as you choose. Just make sure that necessary information, such as your name, address, e-mail address, and phone number, is all on the card. The items will also provide potential employers with a handy means to contact you, rather than wading through a stack of résumés or cover letters.

Remember, anything of true value — like your dream job — is going to require work on your part. It is planning, it is constantly being prepared for your interview, and it is bringing your game face and best apparel to the interview. For all the work you do in advance, and the effort you put into the project, you will be rewarded over and over when you have landed that dream job and can get paid to do something you love. You may not be able to map out your destiny, but you can increase your chances of coming out a winner in the job hunt and hiring process by putting in the effort and persevering.

CHAPTER 11

Conclusion — What to do After You Have Been Hired

Internet Lingo

Digitalized portfolio: A virtual file or folder consisting of various items used to convey your skills and accomplishments to a potential employer. They are visual props used to show, rather than tell, about your expertise.

Microsoft® Visio: A specially designed software program that allows users to create presentations with items such as diagrams, charts, and drawings.

Microsoft PowerPoint®: A program where users can create visual slides that can be used on a computer, printed out, or displayed through a projector for visual and oral presentations.

Visual presentation: A presentation where a projector may be used to show slides, which may accompany an oral presentation.

A new job is always exciting, although it can be stressful and overwhelming at the same time. The first action you should take is to pat yourself on the back for a job well-done.

Without discipline and innovative thinking, strategies, and perseverance, who knows what you would be doing come Monday morning. But your hard work and efforts led you to your new job, and as you are savoring the moment, there are still a few housecleaning tasks to complete as you head off to your new work venture.

Put Your New Internet Skills to Work

Now that you have landed the position, you do not want to just rest on your laurels. You are back in the game. With the new job title comes new opportunities to utilize the skills you have acquired through your Internet job search. Think about all of the procedures you went through during your job hunt. Although some tasks were more difficult than others, you made your way through them all the same.

If you are being training for a position, make sure to take notes — lots of notes. This way, you are not the new person who consistently needs help doing the same task. Also, think about your new skills and how they may be incorporated into the job responsibilities you are being paid to do. Whether you learned how to use **Microsoft Visio** or **PowerPoint**, or how to create your **digitalized** portfolio, ask yourself whether there is a task at your new job that could be done better by using some of these skills that you now have. Say, for example, you have been hired at a company where new projects and project updates are unveiled in monthly meetings. Oral speeches are the only means used to convey the information because the rest of the team is not very savvy when it comes to using computer programs. Why not offer to use your PowerPoint skills to create a **visual presentation** to go with the oral update, or a presentation along with a handout, which you will also prepare using the computer? Imagine how thrilled your new employer will be — not to mention the meeting members who will also be able to not only listen to the project update, but be able to follow its progress visually through the presentation and the handout. This is just one example on how you can really make a name for yourself in your new job.

CASE STUDY: : JOB-SEEKER SHARES ABC'S OF GETTING HIRED AS A TEACHER

Bernadette Milliken, ESL Instructor
Arlington, MA

When educator and English as a Second Language (ESL) instructor Bernadette Milliken wanted to find an additional job, she turned to the Internet as her starting point. While she had been familiar with some computer usage, her experience using it as a job-hunting tool was minimal.

Milliken started her search with Craigslist.org because she had heard it was a good site to use as a job tool, and she was able to find an educational job within her proximity. Although there was contact information for Milliken to submit her résumé and cover letter through the online job advertisement, she opted to take a more personalized approach.

"I just got the information off the job posting, including the company address, the contact person, and the name of the school, and I drove directly over there. I thought that it would be better to submit my application face-to-face," she said. "The personality has to come through, and sometimes it just doesn't on paper."

In addition to personalizing the experience for her employer, Milliken had also prepared in advance just in case the right opportunity surfaced. She had all of her necessary tools ready prior to finding the job posting and applying. In addition to her résumé, the teacher also received online trade magazines to keep abreast of all the new advances and events in the ESL world.

From online trade magazines and Internet research, Milliken took additional steps to ensure success during her job hunt, such as incorporating particular keywords and phrases when designing her résumé and cover letter. But her Internet skills opened up other opportunities for her, too, even after she had been hired.

In the past, Milliken said she has been able to procure private teaching opportunities through the Internet.

"One of my students had encouraged me because of my abilities as an instructor. They thought that I would be good in a one on one situation. I placed ads on Craigslist to teach private ESL lessons to students. I also used a Korean site to find additional students."

Use research skills to stay on top of industry changes

Now that you know where to look for information online, you can put your research skills to work in your new job. Whether you are starting at the bottom of the ladder or as an executive at the top, it does not hurt to stay abreast with the changes taking place in your particular industry.

You know where to find information on both public and private entities. Now you can search the Internet regularly to find out about any significant changes that will impact your job, your company, or the industry. Some sites also allow you the option of signing up for newsletters and updates. You may want to go back to the sites that provided you with the best information to find out whether they offer such information all the time. Also, you can stay in touch, via the Internet, with the various professional contacts you have made through the Internet during your job search journey.

Expand your professional Internet profile

With your new knowledge and your new job, you may want to expand on your professional presence, especially now that you have mastered how to do so. The next time you find yourself in a position of having to secure employment, you may want to save yourself some steps by building on what you have already created. Take, for instance, your professional Internet profile.

You may want to expand your profile by including your new job and the responsibilities you have. This way, you may be in a position to help others, or you may catch the eye of an employer with an even greater job opportunity for the future. It is always easier to maintain what you have than to start from scratch. Continue to add to it, including your new job experiences, accomplishments, and certifications.

Build your network

As you develop and add to your professional Internet presence, you will be able to expand your network, too. Through Internet networking, you have already established relationships with a number of individuals who provided you with valuable information for your new position. Keep up those network connections. When you are working 40 hours a week, it is sometimes difficult to meet individuals who share common professional threads. But Internet networking has made this easier, and by building your professional network, you can offer and provide advice to job seekers like yourself. You can also stay on top of industry changes and other relevant matters by staying connected with the contacts you have made. And, as your presence and network grows, you will make more contacts.

Keep résumés updated

Keeping your résumé updated will require a little thought on your part, but because you have just gone through the experience of designing your document from scratch, it will be easier. As you add new skills to your work repertoire, be sure to eliminate less relevant points of information. Remember: Emphasize your more recent accomplishments and responsibilities, and focus less on older positions. This is true for a chronological résumé or a combination résumé, which includes both your accomplishments and your work experience. In this case, you may not want to drop of the oldest work information, but you may want to delete the tasks or responsibilities that had nothing or little to do with your present and future career path.

Keep track of companies you want to work for

Not everyone ends up with his or her dream job overnight. Sometimes it takes a number of positions and companies before you are really in a work environment you can call home. And while you hustled to find a job this time around, you may have discovered a few companies you would like to work for in the future.

You may want to create a new file folder on your computer desktop titled "Dream Job Companies," or something similar. You can set up job agents if any of the companies allow for such a capacity. This way, you can still remain in the loop about possible openings without having to search job sites or company Web sites. However, visiting those company Web sites may not be a bad idea, either. Sign up for free company newsletters as well, so you stay abreast on the changes that occur. Then, when the time is right, you will be ready for the prefect opportunity because your materials and tools are up-to-speed.

Remember: The sky is the limit with the Internet. Now that you have mastered the Internet job universe, take full advantage of all the opportunities it has to offer. You can map out your career path from beginning to end. You know the tools you will need; you know how to find your way around the electronic world of employment; and you have what it takes to be able to succeed. By putting all of your own talent together with your new knowledge, you are that much closer to finding — and securing — your personal dream job. Your journey begins today.

APPENDIX A

Big-Name Sites, Search Engines, Niche Sites, and Job Boards

Top Job Sites:

- CareerBuilder.com (**www.careerbuilder.com**)

- Craigslist.org (**www.craigslist.org/about/sites**)

- Indeed.com (**www.indeed.com**)

- Monster.com (**www.monster.com**)

- Simplyhired.com (**www.simplyhired.com**)

- USAJobs.gov (**www.usajobs.gov**)

- Yahoo! HotJobs (**http://hotjobs.yahoo.com**)

Other Popular Job Sites:

- Beyond.com (**www.beyond.com**)

- Dice.com (**www.dice.com**)

- Employmentguide.com (**www.employmentguide.com**)

- Hound.com (**www.hound.com**)

- ExecuNet (**www.execunet.com**) – Fee based for executive-level search

- Jobcentral.com (**www.jobcentral.com**)

- Jobs.com (**www.jobs.com**) – Powered by Monster.com

- Jobing.com (**www.jobing.com**)

- Juju.com (**www.job-search-engine.com**)

- Snagajob.com (**www.snagajob.com**)

Niche Job Sites:

- Accounting.com (**www.accounting.com**) – For jobs in the field of accounting

- Administrativejobsite.com (**www.administrativejobsite.com**) – For positions in the administrative and clerical field

- Autojobs.com (**www.autojobs.com**) – For positions in the field of auto mechanics

- Bankjobs.com (**www.bankjobs.com**) – For jobs dealing with the banking and financial industry

- Biotech (**www.biotech.com**) – For positions in the field of biotechnology

- Idealist.org (**www.idealist.org**) – For positions and volunteer opportunities in non-profit groups as well as other institutes and organizations

- Journalismjobs.com (**www.journalismjobs.com**) – For positions in the field of journalism, as well as publishing and writing

- Marketingjobs.com (**www.marketingjobs.com**) – For jobs specifically in the field of marketing

- Medzilla.com (**www.medzilla.com**) – For positions in the health care industry

- Nonprofitjobs.org (**www.nonprofitjobs.org**) – For jobs with non-profit organizations

- Talentzoo.com (**www.talentzoo.com**) – For jobs in the marketing and advertising field

APPENDIX B

Federal and Other Government Job Sites

State-Specific Jobs

While links to states jobs in each state are listed below, another means to find such openings is to visit **www.federaljobssearch.com** and type in the state you are interested in. For example, if you want to find possible positions in state government for Alabama, you may want to type:

www.federaljobsearch.com/Alabama.asp

State Government Sites

If you are looking to pursue a state government position, you may want to visit the specific link to government jobs relative to that particular location. The links below are some that will lead you to state positions. From there, you may want to visit the governor's office via the Internet to find positions, or you can identify a particular state agency you may want to be a part of.

A number of states also require candidates to fill out standardized state job applications. You may want to visit a particular site, fill out the application, and keep in on your desktop for future use if you are thinking of applying to more than one job in that particular state. For example, if you are going to apply to a state government job in Texas, whether you are in El Paso or Dallas or Houston, you will want to first visit **www.twc.state.tx.us/jobs/gvjb/ stateapp.pdf**, where you will be able to download and complete a state application. It can be used for different jobs throughout the state agencies.

Listed below are the Web sites where job opportunities can be found from state to state.

1. Alabama: **https://joblink.alabama.gov/ada/**

2. Alaska: **www.jobs.state.ak.us**

3. Arizona: **https://secure.azstatejobs.gov**

4. Arkansas: **www.ark.org/arstatejobs**

5. California: **www.ca.gov/Employment.html**

6. Colorado: **www.colorado.gov/cs/Satellite/CO-Portal/ CXP/1165693060190**

7. Connecticut: **www.das.state.ct.us/exam/**

8. Delaware: **www.delawarestatejobs.com**

9. Florida: **https://jobs.myflorida.com/index.html**

10. Georgia: **www.georgia.gov/00/channel_ti- tle/0,2094,4802_5037,00.html**

11. Hawaii: **http://hawaii.gov/hrd/main/esd/**

12. Idaho: **http://dhr.idaho.gov/StateJobs/tabid/970/Default.aspx**

13. Illinois: **http://work.illinois.gov/**

14. Indiana: **www.in.gov/spd/**

15. Iowa: **http://das.hre.iowa.gov/state_jobs.html**

16. Kansas: **www.da.ks.gov/ps/aaa/recruitment/**

17. Kentucky: **http://personnel.ky.gov/**

18. Louisiana: **www.civilservice.la.gov/index.asp**

19. Maine: **www.maine.gov/portal/working/jobs.html**

20. Maryland: **www.maryland.gov/working/Pages/working.aspx**

21. Massachusetts: **https://jobs.hrd.state.ma.us/recruit/public/3111/index.do**

22. Michigan: **www.michigan.gov/jobs**

23. Minnesota: **https://statejobs.doer.state.mn.us/JobPosting**

24. Mississippi: **www.mississippi.gov/ms_sub_sub_template.jsp?Category_ID=17**

25. Missouri: **www.mo.gov/Employment/Jobs/**

26. Montana: **http://mt.gov/statejobs/statejobs.asp**

27. Nebraska: **www.wrk4neb.org/**

28. Nevada: **http://dop.nv.gov/**

29. New Hampshire: **http://admin.state.nh.us/hr/**

30. New Jersey: **www.state.nj.us/nj/employ/seekers/**

31. New Mexico: **www.spo.state.nm.us/**

32. New York: **www.cs.state.ny.us/jobseeker/public/**

33. North Carolina: **www.osp.state.nc.us/jobs/**

34. North Dakota: **www.nd.gov/hrms/jobs/announcements.asp**

35. Ohio: **http://careers.ohio.gov/**

36. Oklahoma: **www.ok.gov/opm/State_Jobs/index.html**

37. Oregon: **www.oregonjobs.org/**

38. Pennsylvania: **www.employment.state.pa.us/**

39. Rhode Island: **www.dlt.ri.gov/webdev/JobsRI/StateJobs.htm**

40. South Carolina: **www.ohr.sc.gov/OHR/OHR-jobs-portal-in-dex.phtm**

41. South Dakota: **http://bop.sd.gov/workforus/**

42. Tennessee: **www.tennesseeanytime.org/government/employ-ment.html**

43. Texas: **www.twc.state.tx.us/jobs/job.html**

44. Utah: **www.utah.gov/employment/**

45. Vermont: **www.vermontpersonnel.org/jobapplicant/index.php**

46. Virginia: **http://jobs.state.va.us/**

47. Washington: **www.dop.wa.gov/Pages/DOPHome.aspx**

48. West Virginia: **www.state.wv.us/admin/personnel/jobs/**

49. Wisconsin: **http://wisc.jobs/public/index.asp**

50. Wyoming: **http://personnel.state.wy.us/stjobs/index.htm**

APPENDIX C

Résumé Help and Cover Letter Samples

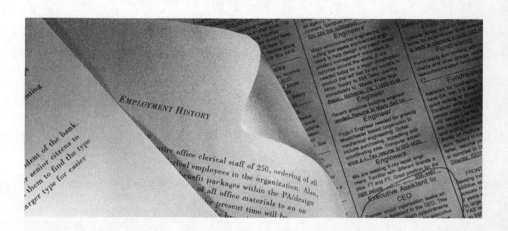

Résumé help

- www.resume-help.org
- www.freeresumehelp.net
- http://jobstar.org/tools/resume/index.php
- www.jobhuntingadvice.com/resume_help.htm
- www.bestsampleresume.com
- www.calltocareer.com
- http://grandresume.com

Sample Résumés

Chronological

Lane Lowe

1 Any Street

Any Town, Any State 00000

(XXX) XXX-XXXX (home)

(XXX) XXX-XXXX (cell)

llowe@gmail.com

SUMMARY

Goal-oriented salesperson who consistently exceeded quota. Diverse retail experience. Management and administrative skills

Experience

Key Holder, Fancy Shop

May 2005 – June 2008

- Helped open new store
- Placed orders to restock merchandise and handled receiving of products
- Managed payroll, scheduling, reports, e-mail, inventory, and records
- Managed new register functions
- Created visual displays and merchandising arrangements

Sales Associate, ABC Department Store - Shoe

August 2001 – May 2005

- Merchandised shoes
- Worked with manufacturer's sales representatives

- Assisted customers fittings
- Worked with department manager on inventory and markdowns

Bartender, Any Watering Hole
January 1999 – August 2001

- Provided customer service in busy sports bar atmosphere
- Managed inventory and ordering
- Was responsible for closing register and supervising cleaning

Education

My Town Community Technical College, Any Town, Any State

Functional

Carolina Covington

(XXX) XXX-XXXX
3510 SE 130th Place
Agoura Hills, CA 91301
carolina.covington@gmail.com

Education

University of Central Florida:

- Bachelor's Degree, Technical Communications, complete in 2010
  - Worked with a team on two occasions to create large handbooks, once as General Editor, once as a Technical Editor
  - Created various business cards and brochures; one brochure is currently in use
  - Skilled in writing, communications, and editing
- Many Creative Writing courses taken, including poetry and fiction workshops

Valencia Community College: Associates Degree, summer 2006

Internship Experience

The Cypress Circle Literary Magazine: Intern poetry editor, fall 2008 through spring 2009

The Florida Reflection Literary Magazine: Intern poetry editor, spring 2008

Job Experience

11/08 – 06/09: Nanny for three boys, ages three, five, and twelve
01/07 – 11/08: First Friends, assistant teacher. Worked mostly in three-year-old and infant room

06/06 – 03/07: Petcountry, salesperson

04/05 – 11/05: Bob Evans, server

04/03 – 04/05: Waterside Village, server

11/03 – 05/04: Café Italia, manager's assistant

References

June Summers, (XXX) XXX-XXXX

Most recent boss; can attest to my work ethic and personality

Dr. Richard Norman, (XXX) XXX-XXXX

English professor I have studied under in two courses; created a grammar handbook in his course ENC 4293

-Portfolio also available-

Combination

EMiLY JONES

emilyjones@ufl.edu
(XXX) XXX-XXXX

3990 W. University Ave.
Gainesville, FL 32607

Education

Aug. 2005 - May 2009

University of Florida, Gainesville, Florida
B.S., Journalism

Print

Jan. 2009 - present

Orange & Blue magazine, University of Florida: Editor-in-Chief
Worked closely with editorial team to manage a 29-person staff of the student-run magazine;
oversaw entire production of 60-page magazine; wrote; edited

Jan. 2008 - May 2008

That Girl! magazine, University of Florida: Editor-in-Chief
Oversaw entire production of class magazine prototype and Web site; organized photo shoots;
supervised art direction; designed; wrote; edited; created original rundowns; assigned stories;
researched competitive sets; submitted TG! to the 2008 Association for Education in Journalism and
Mass Communication Student Magazine Contest and won first place

Aug. 2007 - present

Entertainment magazine, Gainesville, Fla.: Health/Fitness Senior Staff Writer
Tracked a reader's weight-loss in monthly feature "Boot Camp Diary;" brainstormed picture and
box ideas; wrote captions; wrote other articles for Gainesville's No. 1 entertainment magazine

June 2007 - Aug. 2007

The Local Times, Winter Garden, Fla.: Intern
Interviewed; wrote; edited; photographed for local articles about health and entertainment

Fitness

Aug. 2006 - present

The University of Florida, Gainesville, Fla.: Level Three Group Fitness Instructor
Bally Total Fitness, Orlando, Fla.: Group Fitness Instructor, AFAA and BOSU Certified
Planned and taught five to nine classes per week; educated participants about health and fitness;
attended 15th Annual Southeast Collegiate Fitness Expo; participate in cycling, kickboxing, BOSU,
gliding, strength nutrition workshops; recognized as employee of the month on multiple occassions
Formats taught included BOSU, kickboxing, boot camp, cycling, circuit, strength, core and step

Feb. 2009 - present

The University of Florida, Gainesville, Fla.: Mentor, Group Fitness Instructor Training Program
Coached two students throughout the semester in various formats, including BOSU and bootcamp;
critiqued their overall performance as an instructor; gave guidlines and suggestions; followed a
regimented schedule on working with each mentee on all aspects of a workout, including warm up,
creating combinations and breaking them down, and cool down; reviewed interactive instruction;
taught class planning; explained administrative duties

Broadcast

Sept. 2008 - present

TV Station, Gainesville, Fla.: Associate Producer and Student Reporter
Edited shows, wrote scripts and cut VOSOTS with Final Cut Pro and Sienna; created packages;
interviewed; wrote Web articles for the ABC affiliate station; trained in all areas production; reported

Aug. 2008 - present

The Alumni magazine, Gainesville, Fla.: Staff Writer and Assistant Producer
Transcribed and edited for magazine's first video documentary about the Florida FlyIns program; wrote
stories, including a feature story for UF's College of Journalism and Communications alumni magazine

May 2008 - Aug. 2008

TV Station, Orlando, Fla.: Sunrise Reporting Intern
Worked in the field from 3:30 a.m. until noon for the Top 19 market station; wrote Web articles;
interviewed; researched; involved in the Caylee Anthony case; wrote and tracked packages and
stand-ups efficiently for four hours of news on the NBC affiliate

References

Jennifer Gibbs, Orange & Blue: Faculty Adviser
jgibbs@ufl.edu, (XXX) XXX-XXXX

Diane Stevens, UF Department of Recreational Sports: Fitness Coordinator
DianeS@recsports.ufl.edu, (XXX) XXX-XXXX

Target résumé

Amy Tebow
antebow@gmail.com

(XXX) XXX-XXXX

1115 Heisman Ave., Apt No. 1

St. Augustine, FL 32084

EXPERIENCE

The Advisory Company, Chicago, Ill.   October 2008 – May 2009
Copy Editor, Health Group

- Copy edited stories detailing health care issues for several publications by their respective deadlines
- Managed online health policy calendars
- Conducted daily searches of online news sources for stories related to health care policy news

Pricehouse's, Tampa, Fla.   August – September 2008
Contract Copy Editor, Business Practices Division

- Proofread business documents detailing large corporation's best practices
- Incorporated articles detailing new programs and ideas companies to run their businesses more efficiently

Pricehouse's, Tampa, Fla.   June – August 2008
Intern, Editorial Services

- Copy edited documents for the Global Best Practices Web site
- Researched background information to assist writers with their various writing assignments

- Organized Excel spreadsheets detailing each writer and copy editor's projects over a three-month time period

The Gallivanting Gator, Gainesville, Fla.   February - April 2008
  Copy Editor

- Wrote headlines to accompany the articles
- Proofread news stories for AP style, grammar and concision

Creative Planet (The Weekly Loafer), Tampa, Fla. June - August 2006
  Editorial Intern

- Attended movie screenings and wrote film reviews
- Wrote articles on upcoming events that occurred in the greater Tampa Bay area
- Assisted with the annual Best of the Bay issue by archiving previous editions and writing descriptions of businesses named Best of the Bay

EDUCATION

University of Florida, Gainesville Fla.   May 2008
Bachelor of Science in Journalism, Specializing in Editing
Outside Concentration in Education
GPA 3.50/4.00

REFERENCES

Available upon request

Sample Cover Letters

January 1, 2009

Mr. Ben Anderson

Tech Placement Agency

1254 North Atlanta Blvd.

Jacksonville, FL 34875

Dear Mr. Anderson,

It was with great interest that I read about your opening for a full-time reporter on JobWebSiteXYZ.com. The position sounds perfect for someone who enjoys multi-tasking like I do. It is with great enthusiasm that I am submitting my résumé and writing samples for your review.

My experience and skills make me an excellent candidate for this position. I have worked as both a beat reporter for local government covering city and county commission meetings and as a feature reporter for the Living section of my hometown newspaper with a circulation of 25,000 readers.

I enjoyed freelancing while I earned my BS in Journalism from the University of Florida and, thanks to an excellent photo journalism course, I have dabbled in photography and Photoshop editing ever since. I am an avid web browser and even have my own Web site, which you can visit at **www.clipsandphotoexamples.website**.

I believe that I am well-qualified for this position, and I believe you will agree after you read the sample I have included. I hope we have an opportunity to meet in person to further discuss the details of this job opening.

Sincerely,

Janet Smith

Trisha Smith
301 West Peach Tree St.
Atlanta, GA 48273
(XXX) XXX-XXXX

Dear Sir/Ma'am:

After working 12 years for a small family-run insurance company, I find myself looking for new employment. The wonderful owner passed away, and the family has decided not to continue the business he started. I worked as his bookkeeper and administrative assistant from the time I graduated with my bachelor's from the University of Georgia until now.

While his passing is a great loss for me, it is with excitement I embark on my quest for a new job. I am detail-oriented, keeping perfect books the entire time I worked at my current position (which held up to the close scrutiny of an IRS audit in 2002). I am an excellent multi-tasker, managing my duties as a mother of two boys and my employer's busy office schedule. I'm a self-starter who doesn't need to be asked to fill a need — I simply get things done.

My résumé is listed detailing my skills and accomplishments, but I would enjoy speaking with any interested parties in greater length about how I can assist their office like I did for so many years for my former employer.

Regards,

Trisha Smith

APPENDIX D

Career Aptitude Tests and Links

Career Aptitude Test Links

- www.funeducation.com

- www.careercolleges.com/career-assessment-test.jsp

- www.careercolleges.com/career-assessment-test.jsp

- www.career-tests-guide.com/career-aptitude-tests.html

- www.careertypes.com

- www.career-tests-guide.com/career-aptitude-tests.html

- www.colorwize.com

- www.questcareer.com/career_assessment_resources.html

BIBLIOGRAPHY

*Sources used in additional to online materials referenced in the Appendices.

Bavol, Todd, The Job Search Ninja.

Bolles, Mark Emery and Richard Nelson Bolles, Job-Hunting Online, Berkeley, CA, 2005.

Dikel, Margaret Riley, Frances E. Rohm, Guide to Internet Job Searching, US, 2008.

Doyle, Alison, the About.com guide to Job Searching, Avon, MA.

Doyle, Alison, Internet Your Way to a New Job, Cupertino, CA 2008.

McClure, John, Get the Job You Want, Kissimmee, FL, 2008.

AUTHOR BIOGRAPHY

Janet Nagle is a writer out of San Antonio, Texas, where she moved after spending nearly a decade in the media industry in Massachusetts. In addition to working as a journalist, news and features editor, and managing editor for several daily and weekly publications, she worked in the Massachusetts House of Representatives and the State Senate, as well as in one of the Governor's Cabinet Secretariats.

While working in state government, Nagle served as the employer relations manager for the Massachusetts Department of Transitional Assistance. Her job was to meet with potential employers and secure job slots for a subsidized wage program. She has also worked as a writer for a Texas magazine and for Examiner.com.

She is a former member of the Romance Writers of America (RWA), the San Antonio Writers Meetup Group, the San Antonio Romance Authors (SARA), and the San Antonio Writers Guild (SAWG).

INDEX